I0822531

The Art of War

The Timeless Guide to Strategy, Leadership, and Victory

A Modern Translation

Adapted for the Contemporary Reader

Sun Tzu

Translated by Tim Zengerink

Table of Contents

Preface - Message to the Reader

Rebuilding the Greatest Library in Human History

Thousands of years ago, the Library of Alexandria was the heart of global knowledge — until it was lost.

Now, we're rebuilding it — and you're invited to join.

At the Modern Library of Alexandria, our mission is simple: make *every book* available to *every person*, in every language, format, and edition.

Here's how we do it:

- **Deluxe Print Editions at True Printing Cost** - Order paperbacks, hardcovers, or boxsets at the exact printing cost — no markup.
- **Unlimited Access to the Greatest Works** - Explore thousands of timeless classics in modern eBook and audiobook editions. Free for every reader, everywhere.
- **Modern Translations for Every Language & Dialect** -Clear, accessible versions of the world's greatest works, translated into every language and dialect.

When you visit **LibraryofAlexandria.com**, you're not just accessing books — you're joining a global movement to restore, preserve, and share the wisdom of civilization.

Join us today at LibraryofAlexandria.com

Together, we'll ensure the light of human wisdom never fades again.

With gratitude,

The Modern Library of Alexandria Team

Visit:

www.libraryofalexandria.com

Or scan the code below:

Introduction

I. Brief Biography of Sun Tzu

Origins and Early Life

Sun Tzu, originally named Sun Wu, was born around 544 BCE in the state of Qi, which is now part of Shandong, China. The name Sun Tzu, by which he is better known, is a title meaning "Master Sun." Though much of his early life is still unknown, historical evidence suggests he came from a family with strong roots in military strategy and learning. This background likely helped shape his extraordinary skills in warfare and tactics, setting him up for the distinguished career he would later have.

As a young man, Sun Tzu began gaining a reputation for his sharp mind in strategy, though historical records about him are somewhat scarce. The lack of solid information has only made his life more fascinating, with parts of his story seeming like a mix of history and legend. His eventual rise to fame as a general and thinker was based not just on his practical knowledge of warfare, but also his ability to apply general ideas to real-life situations. His famous work, *The Art of War*, would form the foundation of his lasting influence, even though much of his life story has been blended with myths.

Military Career and Rise to Prominence

Sun Tzu's skills in military strategy didn't go unnoticed. He served under King Helü of the state of Wu, a role that gave him the chance to show his expertise on a larger stage. His ability to turn hopeless situations into victories earned him respect across the region. One of the biggest examples of his brilliance was when he defeated the state of Chu, which was much bigger and had more resources. This win highlighted his talent for outsmarting opponents with greater numbers and supplies.

The defeat of Chu was more than just a military win; it strengthened Wu's power and stability during a time when warfare between Chinese states was constant. Sun Tzu's strategies often used psychological tricks and deception, with clever tactics to weaken his enemies' morale before any fighting began. His deep understanding of terrain, human nature, and the use of deception made him stand out among other military minds of his time. These achievements earned him lasting fame and confirmed his place as one of the greatest military strategists in Chinese history.

Creation of The Art of War

It was during this period of political upheaval and near-constant warfare that Sun Tzu is believed to have authored The Art of War. The Warring States period (475–221 BCE) was a time of great instability, with

various factions vying for control of China. In this context, Sun Tzu's strategies and insights were not only revolutionary but essential for survival.

Rather than a theoretical treatise, The Art of War is a distilled collection of Sun Tzu's accumulated experiences and the military wisdom passed down from generations before him. The text, composed of concise aphorisms and principles, is a practical guide intended for military leaders facing the challenges of warfare. Sun Tzu's approach to warfare emphasized the importance of strategy over brute force, and many of his insights remain highly applicable even in the modern world. His genius lay in his ability to condense complex concepts into simple, memorable phrases that have stood the test of time.

Even today, The Art of War continues to influence a wide array of fields beyond the battlefield, from business to sports, and remains a touchstone for anyone seeking to understand the nature of conflict and strategy. The timelessness of Sun Tzu's work speaks to his mastery of the art of warfare and his ability to provide wisdom that transcends the ages.

II. Historical Context

Sun Tzu lived during one of the most chaotic times in Chinese history, a period historians call the Spring and Autumn period, which later became the Warring States period (around 771–221 BCE). This era saw the weakening of the Zhou Dynasty's power, leading to constant wars between rival states. Regional leaders fought for control, with alliances constantly shifting and battles happening frequently. The political scene was unstable, and military skill was vital not just for winning but for survival.

As states competed for dominance, warfare was about more than just expanding territories; it was necessary for keeping sovereignty. Even small mistakes could lead to the complete destruction of a state, making military leaders crucial to the survival of nations. It was in this intense environment that Sun Tzu's strategies developed. He created his tactics not only to secure victories but to ensure long-term survival in a world where states were often annexed or destroyed. His strategies responded to a reality where the stakes were incredibly high, offering insights that went beyond war and into the political dynamics of the time.

The fierce competition for power among Chinese states during the Warring States period required new approaches to warfare, focusing on cunning, intelligence, and strategy rather than just raw strength. Sun

Tzu's writings came out of this era of near-constant conflict, where he understood that success depended on outsmarting the opponent, not just overpowering them. His methods were designed for a time when a single wrong move could lead to disaster, stressing careful planning and the need for preparation in an unpredictable and dangerous world.

The Role of Warfare in Ancient China

In ancient China, warfare was much more than just battles fought on the field; it was closely connected with politics, philosophy, and governance. Leaders during this time were expected not only to be skilled in battle but also to be strong in diplomacy and statecraft. Military action was often a tool used to achieve political goals, and leaders had to balance the challenges of internal governance while also preparing for outside threats. Sun Tzu's approach to warfare reflects this larger understanding, as he constantly stressed the importance of planning ahead, being flexible, and understanding both the enemy and one's own forces.

Warfare during this period was all-encompassing. It involved logistics, governance, and diplomacy, areas where military leaders needed to show not only strength but also wisdom. Sun Tzu's strategies, which often focused on winning without fighting, came from this broader view of conflict, where preserving resources and maintaining the stability of the state were as crucial as defeating the enemy. His well-known principle, "The supreme art of war is to subdue the enemy without fighting," demonstrates his understanding of the long-term effects of war. Instead of seeking short-term victories at great costs, he promoted strategies that would protect the state's power while weakening the opponent's will.

During Sun Tzu's era, military leaders were expected to grasp the moral and philosophical sides of warfare. Confucian values influenced Chinese society deeply, shaping how rulers led and how they fought. Leaders were judged not just by their military successes but by their ability to keep order and promote justice. Sun Tzu's work reflects this, as it puts great importance on the qualities of leadership and the ethical aspects of warfare. He supported the idea of a wise and virtuous leader, one who could inspire loyalty among soldiers while staying calm and focused in the chaos of battle.

The political landscape was always changing, with alliances breaking as quickly as they were formed. Espionage, deception, and psychological warfare became key tools for staying ahead. Sun Tzu's contributions to the art of war went beyond just battlefield tactics; they involved understanding the enemy's mind and manipulating both physical and mental conditions to achieve victory. He understood that sometimes the best battle is the one that's won before it even starts. His insights into psychological manipulation, deception, and moral unity within an army were direct responses to the complex and high-stakes world of ancient Chinese warfare.

In this world of shifting power and constant conflict, Sun Tzu developed his principles not as abstract ideas but as practical tools for survival and dominance. His belief that victory could be achieved in ways other than battle was groundbreaking in a time when brute strength often ruled. His strategies focused on flexibility, intelligence, and the power of unpredictability. By continuously adjusting to changing situations, he believed a general could turn even the most desperate circumstances into opportunities for success. In this way, his work is not only a reflection of his era but a timeless guide for those looking to navigate conflict with wisdom and precision.

III. Philosophical Background

Sun Tzu's ideas didn't develop in isolation; they were influenced by the major philosophical traditions of ancient China, especially Daoism and Confucianism. Daoism, which emphasizes balance, harmony, and non-contention, had a deep impact on his strategic thinking. At its core, Daoism teaches that one should move with the natural flow of the universe, rather than resist it. This belief in flexibility and adaptability is reflected in Sun Tzu's view that a good leader must be flexible in both thought and action, ready to adapt to changing situations instead of sticking rigidly to a set plan. The idea of winning with minimal force—ideally without fighting at all—embodies the Daoist principle of achieving results with the least effort, which is central to The Art of War.

Moreover, Daoism's focus on harmony is seen in Sun Tzu's approach to warfare as an art where the best outcomes are those that avoid conflict altogether. He recognized that forcing a victory often brings about unnecessary destruction and loss, not just in terms of lives but also resources and morale. Instead, he advocated for strategies that involved subtlety, psychological manipulation, and careful planning, all aligned with the natural course of events. Sun Tzu's famous saying, "The supreme art of war is to subdue the enemy without fighting," reflects Daoist wisdom, where the soft overcomes the hard, and the flexible triumphs over the rigid.

Confucianism also played a key role in shaping Sun Tzu's philosophy. Confucian values like duty, ethical conduct, and governing with moral integrity are present in his view of leadership. In Confucian thought, a leader's role is not just about winning; it includes the well-being of the people and the pursuit of order and justice. Sun Tzu's writings, although focused on military strategy, emphasize that a good general must also be a wise and virtuous leader. This aligns with the Confucian ideal of the "Junzi," or the gentleman, who leads by moral virtue and serves as a role model. Sun Tzu believed that an effective leader earns loyalty and trust, not through fear or force, but through wisdom, fairness, and calm decision-making. The combination of Confucian ethics and Daoist practicality creates a balanced framework for Sun Tzu's strategies, making The Art of War not just a guide to military success but also a blueprint for ethical leadership.

Core Principles of Sun Tzu's Philosophy: The Importance of Strategy Over Force

At the core of Sun Tzu's philosophy is the belief that strategic insight is more valuable than brute strength. He argues that the best victories are those achieved without fighting, highlighting the need for careful planning, foresight, and the use of intelligence rather than relying solely on physical power. For Sun Tzu, a leader's role is to outthink their opponent instead of outfight them. He advocated for a strategic approach that reduces the costs of war, both in terms of human lives and resources. Instead of direct conflict, Sun Tzu advises military leaders to disorient their enemies, target their weaknesses, and use deception to gain an advantage. To him, a well-fought battle is one that ends before it even starts, with the enemy defeated by the unseen forces of superior strategy.

Flexibility and Adaptability in Warfare

One of Sun Tzu's key principles is that rigid plans often lead to failure. Success on the battlefield depends on the ability to adapt and respond to constantly changing conditions. He teaches that no two battles are the same, so no single strategy can work for every situation. Instead, Sun Tzu emphasizes the need for flexibility, urging generals to stay fluid in both thought and action. In his view, the best leaders are those who can read the terrain, understand their troops' morale, anticipate their enemy's moves, and adjust their tactics as needed. By avoiding predictable patterns, a leader can keep their opponents off balance, staying one step ahead.

Flexibility goes beyond just physical movements on the battlefield. It includes mental agility, the ability to think quickly, and the willingness to abandon a failing plan for a better one. Sun Tzu believed that sticking stubbornly to a plan, no matter how well thought out, could lead to disaster if it didn't fit the situation. His philosophy encourages leaders to be like water, adapting to the shape of their environment, changing form as conditions change, and always finding a way to move forward. This principle of adaptability has made The Art of War highly relevant in many areas beyond the military, including business and sports, where the ability to pivot in response to new challenges is often the key to success.

Psychological Warfare

Another core element of Sun Tzu's philosophy is his deep understanding of the human mind, both in terms of the enemy and one's own troops. He places great emphasis on psychological warfare, believing that many battles are won or lost in the mind long before they are fought on the battlefield. A leader who can demoralize the enemy, spread confusion, or instill doubt has already set the stage for victory. Sun Tzu advocates using tactics such as deception, misinformation, and surprise to weaken the enemy's confidence and will to fight. By showing strength when weak or pretending to be disorganized when ready to attack, a leader can manipulate the enemy into making costly errors. To Sun Tzu, deception is not just a tactic—it is the essence of warfare.

Equally important is understanding the psychology of one's own troops. Sun Tzu teaches that a successful leader must know how to keep their forces united and their morale high. Soldiers who trust their commander, believe in their cause, and feel confident in the strategy are far more likely to fight bravely and with determination. Sun Tzu believed that a wise general knows how to inspire and motivate, how to reward loyalty, and how to manage fear and uncertainty within the ranks. In his view, leadership is just as much about fostering the right mindset as it is about military skill.

The Role of Leadership

At the core of Sun Tzu's strategic thought lies Sun Tzu believed that leadership is essential to the success of any endeavor, whether military or otherwise. The qualities of a great leader, in his view, go beyond tactical skill. A leader must possess wisdom, remain calm under pressure, be decisive, and uphold moral integrity. For Sun Tzu, leadership isn't just about giving orders; it's about guiding one's people with a steady hand and clear vision. The ability of a leader to inspire trust and unity among their troops is often the key to determining the outcome of a battle.

In The Art of War, Sun Tzu stresses that a leader must deeply understand human nature and manage both resources and emotions wisely. A good leader knows when to be strict and when to show compassion, when to give rewards and when to administer punishment, always balancing authority with wisdom. The leader's role is to create harmony within the ranks, ensuring that everyone, from the highest officers to the lowest soldiers, works together as a unified team. Sun Tzu believed that leadership was the ultimate factor in determining success, and that no amount of strength or resources could make up for a lack of vision and guidance from the top.

For Sun Tzu, leadership is both an art and a responsibility. It requires not only the skill to create great strategies but also the wisdom to carry them out with compassion and integrity. His insights elevate the role of a leader to that of a moral authority, making it clear that true power comes not from dominance but from understanding and mastering oneself, the situation, and those who follow.

IV. Key Themes and Structure of The Art of War

The Art of Strategy

At the core of The Art of War is the idea that victory is achieved through careful planning and strategic foresight. Instead of depending on brute force or sheer numbers, Sun Tzu highlights the importance of intelligence, preparation, and the thoughtful management of resources. To him, a successful campaign begins long before the actual battle. It requires a leader to evaluate not only their own strengths and weaknesses but also those of their enemy. This involves understanding the terrain, the morale of the troops, and the timing of actions. A well-planned strategy, in Sun Tzu's view, allows one to control the battlefield before the enemy even realizes they are being outmaneuvered.

Sun Tzu explains that strategy is the key to using minimal resources for maximum effect. It's not enough to simply fight well; one must fight smart, knowing when to strike and when to hold back. His focus on strategic thinking teaches that victory often belongs to those who understand when to avoid fighting altogether. For Sun Tzu, the greatest generals are those who can win wars without engaging in combat. His insights encourage readers to look at the bigger picture of their challenges, whether in warfare or life, and to approach them with deliberate, calculated actions rather than reacting on impulse.

The Principle of Deception

One of the most enduring and thought-provoking principles in The Art of War is the role of deception. Sun Tzu's famous statement, "All warfare is based on deception," sums up his belief that a commander's true strength lies in their ability to mislead and outsmart the enemy. Deception isn't just a tactic—it's a fundamental part of strategy, allowing a leader to shape the enemy's perceptions and decisions. By creating a false sense of security or concealing one's true intentions, a skilled leader can manipulate their adversary into making costly errors. Misinformation, fake retreats, and surprise attacks are all tools in the strategist's toolkit.

In Sun Tzu's philosophy, deception is about gaining the upper hand through psychological means. The aim is to make the opponent feel secure where they are weak and vulnerable where they are strong. By hiding one's true strengths and revealing only what is necessary, a general can keep the enemy in a constant state of doubt. This unpredictability, according to Sun Tzu, is essential for achieving success. His teachings on deception go far beyond the battlefield and have proven valuable in many areas of modern life, including business negotiations, competitive sports, and political strategy.

Adaptability and Flexibility

Throughout The Art of War, Sun Tzu consistently emphasizes the importance of adaptability in the face of changing circumstances. A leader who clings to a single plan or strategy, regardless of the evolving situation, is bound to fail. Instead, Sun Tzu advocates for a flexible approach, where a commander can pivot quickly and seize opportunities as they arise. In his view, the ability to adapt is a defining quality of a great general. Sun Tzu compares the ideal leader to water, which conforms to the shape of whatever contains it. Just as water flows around obstacles, a successful commander must move with the ever-changing conditions of warfare.

This principle of adaptability aligns with Sun Tzu's belief that no two battles are alike. The unpredictable nature of conflict requires a mindset open to change, whether in tactics, alliances, or terrain. Leaders must be able to set aside preconceived notions and embrace the fluid nature of their surroundings. Sun Tzu's insight extends beyond military situations to modern leadership challenges, reminding readers that success often depends on staying flexible, innovative, and responsive to new information.

The Role of Morale and Unity

For Sun Tzu, victory is not merely about having the largest army or the most skilled fighters. The morale of the troops and the unity of the command structure are just as vital to success as any weapon or strategy. Soldiers who trust their leader and believe in their cause are much more likely to perform well under pressure than those who are demoralized or divided. Sun Tzu places significant importance on treating soldiers with respect, addressing their needs, and inspiring them with a sense of purpose. A general who can command loyalty and cultivate unity within the ranks is far better prepared to face the challenges of war.

Additionally, Sun Tzu underscores the need for clear and consistent leadership. A general must be decisive and fair, maintaining discipline while also knowing when to show compassion. The bond between a leader and their soldiers is a crucial element in creating a cohesive and effective fighting force. Internal harmony can often be the deciding factor in battle, especially when facing difficult circumstances. Sun Tzu's teachings on morale and unity go beyond the battlefield, offering valuable insights for modern leaders in business, politics, or personal endeavors. They remind us that a team's success often hinges as much on its internal dynamics as it does on external factors.

V. Influence and Legacy of The Art of War

Influence in East Asia

The Art of War has been a foundational text in East Asia for centuries, deeply influencing the philosophies and practices of military leaders, scholars, and political strategists. From China to Japan and Korea, its principles have shaped the ways wars were fought and how empires were governed. In China, where Sun Tzu first developed his strategies, dynasties studied the text to refine their military tactics, using its teachings to defend and expand their territories. Beyond the battlefield, The Art of War guided Chinese governance, diplomacy, and statecraft, serving as a manual for leaders who sought to balance power, strategy, and ethics.

In Japan, The Art of War became prominent during the Samurai era, especially in the development of

Bushido, the warrior's code of honor. Japanese military leaders, including figures like Oda Nobunaga and Tokugawa Ieyasu, drew inspiration from Sun Tzu's principles. His teachings on discipline, adaptability, and the importance of psychological warfare resonated deeply with the samurai ethos, further embedding The Art of War into Japan's cultural and military traditions. The text's influence reached beyond warfare, shaping how political leaders approached negotiations and alliances.

Korea also embraced Sun Tzu's strategies, applying them in times of internal conflict and external threats, particularly during struggles with neighboring states. For centuries, Korean scholars and military generals turned to The Art of War when planning defenses and military campaigns, finding in its pages the strategic insight and adaptability needed to navigate complex geopolitical landscapes. Sun Tzu's focus on intelligence, deception, and strategic positioning over brute force made his work a vital resource in East Asia's long history of warfare and statecraft.

Influence in Modern Warfare

As the centuries went by, The Art of War spread beyond East Asia and started to influence military strategies around the world. Its ideas were eventually adopted by Western military leaders and strategists, especially during the 19th and 20th centuries when warfare became more complicated. For example, Napoleon Bonaparte is said to have been greatly influenced by Sun Tzu's teachings. His military campaigns across Europe showed how effective it was to use strategic surprise, careful planning, and taking advantage of the enemy's weaknesses—all key elements of Sun Tzu's approach.

In the 20th century, Sun Tzu's influence could be seen especially in guerrilla warfare tactics. Revolutionary leaders like Mao Zedong in China and Ho Chi Minh in Vietnam used The Art of War's focus on psychological warfare, deception, and asymmetrical tactics to defeat stronger and better-equipped enemies. In Vietnam, during the conflict with the United States, Ho Chi Minh and his generals applied Sun Tzu's strategies very effectively, using the jungle terrain and psychological endurance to weaken their enemy's determination and eventually force their withdrawal.

Today, The Art of War is often studied in military academies alongside other classic works on strategy and tactics. Its ideas have shaped both the theoretical and practical education of military officers around the world. From Sandhurst in the UK to West Point in the United States, Sun Tzu's teachings still provide important lessons about leadership, intelligence gathering, and the moral aspects of warfare. His belief that the best victories are those won without fighting connects well with modern military thinking, where political and economic strategies often work alongside or instead of traditional battles.

Beyond the Battlefield: Business, Sports, and Politics

While The Art of War started as a military guide, its influence has spread far beyond the battlefield. In the business world, leaders and entrepreneurs have used Sun Tzu's principles to navigate competitive markets, secure good deals, and manage teams effectively. The strategic use of resources, understanding the competition, and adapting to changes are all ideas from The Art of War that have been applied to the corporate world. Today, it's common for business executives to look to Sun Tzu for advice on everything from launching new products to negotiating mergers.

Likewise, sports coaches and athletes have found value in Sun Tzu's focus on preparation, adaptability, and mental strength. Competitive sports, like warfare, require knowing your opponent, anticipating their moves, and adjusting strategies as the game goes on. Whether in battle or in sports, the ability to stay calm and outsmart the competition is universally important.

In politics, The Art of War has also left its mark. Leaders use its ideas when approaching diplomacy, forming alliances, and even running election campaigns. Politicians often apply Sun Tzu's tactics to influence public perception, undermine rivals without direct conflict, and take advantage of timing and positioning. The text's focus on intelligence gathering and strategic alliances is especially relevant in modern politics, where behind-the-scenes efforts can determine the outcome of public contests.

A Lasting Legacy

The Art of War remains a timeless resource, providing guidance that transcends time, culture, and discipline. Whether on the battlefield, in the boardroom, or in everyday life, Sun Tzu's strategies have endured because they are rooted in a deep understanding of human nature and the complexities of conflict. His ability to simplify the chaotic and often harsh realities of war into clear, actionable principles continues to inspire leaders across various fields.

As we move further into an age where technology and information play increasingly larger roles in conflict and competition, Sun Tzu's teachings on deception, intelligence, and adaptability feel more relevant than ever. His insights remind us that victory is not always achieved through strength alone, but through careful thought, ethical leadership, and a deep understanding of the human element in every pursuit.

Sun Tzu's influence on both ancient and modern warfare, along with his broader impact on business, politics, and leadership, solidifies The Art of War as one of the most important and lasting texts on strategy. His legacy continues to shape how people approach conflict, competition, and success, offering timeless wisdom that resonates with each generation.

Chapter 1 - Laying Plans

Sun Tzu said: The art of war is critically important to the State. It can be the difference between life and death, leading to either safety or ruin. Therefore, it must always be carefully studied and never ignored.

The art of war is based on five key factors that must be considered in every military decision. These factors are: (1) The Moral Law; (2) Heaven; (3) Earth; (4) The Commander; (5) Method and discipline.

The Moral Law ensures that the people are fully united with their ruler, making them willing to follow him, even risking their lives without fear of danger.

Heaven refers to the natural conditions, like day and night, cold and heat, and the changing of seasons.

Earth involves distances, both large and small, areas of safety and danger, wide open spaces and narrow paths, and the possibilities of survival or death.

The Commander represents the qualities of wisdom, honesty, kindness, courage, and strictness.

Method and discipline cover the organization of the army, the ranks, the roles assigned to each soldier, and the control of supplies and resources.

These five factors must be studied in depth by those who seek to understand the art of war. By mastering them, a ruler can win the loyalty of the people and command a strong, unified army capable of facing any challenge.

The Moral Law creates harmony between the ruler and the people, inspiring them to follow without hesitation, even in the face of great danger.

Heaven includes the cycles of day and night, the changes in temperature, and the timing of seasons. Some interpret this as a reflection of the broader workings of nature, like the balance of forces or natural elements.

Earth includes not just physical distances but also the dangers and safety that different terrains bring, whether they are wide open plains or narrow mountain passes. These elements can determine the chances of survival or death.

The Commander stands for qualities that inspire trust and loyalty—wisdom, honesty, kindness, bravery, and firmness in discipline. These virtues are essential for strong leadership.

Finally, Method and discipline ensure that the army is well-organized, with clear roles and responsibilities, and that resources are well-managed. These elements ensure that the military is prepared for anything and that chaos is avoided during battle.

Method and discipline mean organizing the army into its proper divisions, assigning ranks among the officers, maintaining roads to ensure supplies can reach the army, and controlling military spending.

These five principles should be well-known to every general: the one who knows them will be victorious; the one who does not will fail.

Therefore, in your planning, when trying to understand the military situation, use these principles as the basis of comparison, in this way:

Which of the two rulers follows the Moral Law? (That is, who is in harmony with their people?)

Which of the two generals is more skilled?

Who has the advantage of favorable conditions from Heaven and Earth?

On which side is discipline enforced the most strictly? (There is a story about Ts'ao Ts'ao, a strict disciplinarian who once followed his own rule so closely that he sentenced himself to death for letting his horse damage crops. Instead of execution, he was convinced to cut off his hair as punishment.)

Which army is stronger, both in physical strength and spirit?

Which side has officers and soldiers who are better trained? (Wang Tzŭ once said that without constant practice, officers will hesitate when forming for battle, and without constant practice, the general will be uncertain when a crisis comes.)

Which side has greater consistency in rewarding good actions and punishing bad behavior?

By considering these seven points, I can predict who will win or lose.

The general who listens to my advice and acts on it will win: such a person should be kept in command! The general who ignores my advice and does not act on it will be defeated: such a person should be dismissed!

While you follow my advice for success, also take advantage of any favorable circumstances that go beyond the usual rules.

As circumstances change, you should adjust your plans accordingly. (Sun Tzu, as a practical soldier, rejects rigid reliance on theoretical principles. He warns us not to rely too heavily on abstract rules because, as Chang Yu says, while the basic principles of strategy can be explained clearly, you must adapt to the enemy's actions to secure a favorable position in battle. Before the Battle of Waterloo, Lord Uxbridge, commanding the cavalry, went to the Duke of Wellington to ask about his plans for the next day. He explained that if he suddenly had to take command, he would need to know the plans. The Duke listened quietly and asked, "Who will attack first tomorrow—me or Bonaparte?" Uxbridge answered, "Bonaparte." "Well," replied the Duke, "Bonaparte hasn't told me his plans, and since my strategy depends on his, how can you expect me to tell you mine?")

All warfare is based on deception. (This wise and profound statement is acknowledged by all soldiers. Col. Henderson notes that Wellington, known for many military qualities, was especially skilled in hiding his movements and deceiving both friend and foe.)

When we are able to attack, we must make it seem as though we are not ready; when using our forces, we must appear inactive; when we are near, we must make the enemy believe we are far away; and when we are far away, we must make him believe we are close by.

Lure the enemy with baits. Pretend to be in disarray, and then crush him. (Most commentators, except Chang Yu, interpret this as "when he is disorganized, crush him," but it's more natural to understand this as another example of how deception works in war.)

If the enemy is well-prepared at all points, be ready for him. If he is stronger, avoid him.

If your opponent has a bad temper, provoke him. Pretend to be weak so that he becomes overconfident. (Wang Tzŭ, as quoted by Tu Yu, compares this tactic to how a cat plays with a mouse, pretending to be weak before suddenly striking.)

If the enemy is resting, don't let him have peace. (This likely means to keep up pressure on the enemy, although Mei Yao-ch'en suggests it could mean "while we rest, let the enemy exhaust himself." The Yu Lan interprets it as "lure him on and tire him out.")

If his forces are united, divide them. (Many commentators offer an alternative explanation: "If the ruler and his subjects are in harmony, cause division between them.")

Attack the enemy where he is unprepared; appear in places where you are not expected.

These military strategies that lead to victory must not be revealed in advance.

A general who wins a battle makes many calculations in his temple before the battle begins. (Chang Yu notes that in ancient times, a temple was set aside for a general about to lead an army, where he could carefully plan his campaign.)

On the other hand, a general who loses a battle makes few calculations ahead of time. Thus, many calculations lead to victory, while few calculations lead to defeat. How much worse it is when no calculations are made at all! It is through understanding this that I can predict who is likely to win or lose.

Chapter 2 - Waging War

Ts'ao Kung comments: "He who wishes to fight must first calculate the cost," which prepares us for the realization that this chapter is not primarily about what we might expect from its title, but is instead focused on the planning of resources and strategies.

Sun Tzu said: In warfare, when there are in the field a thousand swift chariots, an equal number of heavy chariots, and a hundred thousand soldiers clad in armor (the swift chariots were lightly built and, according to Chang Yu, were used for attack; the heavy chariots were stronger and designed for defense. Li Ch'uan suggests that the heavy chariots were also light, but this seems unlikely. It's interesting to note the similarities between early Chinese warfare and that of the Homeric Greeks. In both cases, the war chariot was central to military formation, surrounded by groups of foot soldiers. As for the numbers here, it is said that each swift chariot was accompanied by 75 footmen, and each heavy chariot by 25 footmen, dividing the army into a thousand battalions, each consisting of two chariots and a hundred men), with provisions sufficient to sustain them for a thousand li (2.78 modern li make up a mile, though the length may have varied somewhat since Sun Tzu's time), the total daily expenditure, both at home and at the front—including the entertainment of guests, small items like glue and paint, and the sums spent on chariots and armor—will amount to a thousand ounces of silver per day. This is the cost of maintaining an army of 100,000 men.

When you engage in actual combat, if victory is slow to come, the soldiers' weapons will grow dull, and their enthusiasm will fade. If you lay siege to a town, you will drain your strength.

Additionally, if the campaign is prolonged, the state's resources will not be able to bear the strain.

Now, when your weapons are dulled, your enthusiasm has waned, your strength is drained, and your resources are depleted, other leaders will rise to exploit your vulnerability. At that point, no one, no matter how wise, will be able to prevent the inevitable consequences.

Thus, while we have heard of foolish haste in war, cleverness has never been associated with long delays. (This brief and challenging sentence has puzzled commentators. Ts'ao Kung, Li Ch'uan, Meng Shih, Tu Yu, Tu Mu, and Mei Yao-ch'en all comment that a general, though typically unwise, might still win by sheer speed. Ho Shih adds that while haste may be foolish, it at least saves energy and resources, whereas prolonged campaigns, even if skillful, lead to disaster. Wang Hsi avoids the difficulty by saying that lengthy operations age the army, drain wealth, empty the treasury, and bring suffering to the people; true cleverness avoids these pitfalls. Chang Yu argues that as long as victory is possible, even hasty actions are preferable to overly cautious delays. However, Sun Tzu does not explicitly suggest that ill-considered haste is better than well-thought-out but prolonged strategies. Instead, his point is more cautious: while speed may sometimes be unwise, delays are always foolish, if only because they lead to national impoverishment. When considering Sun Tzu's point, the example of Fabius Cunctator inevitably comes to mind. Fabius deliberately measured the endurance of Rome against Hannibal's isolated army, reasoning that Hannibal would suffer more in a prolonged campaign in foreign territory. However, whether Fabius' strategy would have worked in the long run is debatable. Though the reversal of his approach led to the disaster at Cannae, this only suggests a negative presumption in favor of his tactics.)

Only someone who fully understands the horrors of war can fully comprehend the value of conducting it in a profitable manner. (That is, with speed. Only those who recognize the devastating consequences of a long war can truly grasp the supreme importance of bringing it to a swift conclusion. Although only two commentators favor this interpretation, it fits the logic of the context better than the alternative rendering, "He who does not know the evils of war cannot appreciate its benefits," which is clearly pointless.)

The skillful commander does not call for a second levy, nor are his supply wagons loaded more than twice. (Once war begins, he will not waste valuable time waiting for reinforcements, nor will he retreat to gather fresh supplies, but will instead cross the enemy's border without delay. While this may seem like a bold strategy, history's greatest military leaders, from Julius Caesar to Napoleon Bonaparte, have all emphasized the importance of time—that is, being slightly ahead of the enemy—over numerical superiority or careful logistical calculations.)

Bring war materials from home, but rely on the enemy for provisions. In this way, the army will always have enough food to meet its needs. (The Chinese word translated here as "war material" literally means "things to be used" and is understood in the broadest sense. It includes everything needed by the army, except for food.)

When the state treasury is poor, the army must be supported by contributions from far-off places. Relying on distant sources to sustain the army leads to impoverishment of the people.

The beginning of this sentence does not connect smoothly with the next, though it is clearly meant to do so. The arrangement is so awkward that it suggests some corruption in the text. It rarely occurs to Chinese commentators that an amendment might be needed to clarify the meaning, so they offer no help here. The Chinese words Sun Tzu used to indicate the cause of the people's impoverishment refer to a system where farmers sent their corn directly to the army. But why would it fall to them to maintain the army in this way, unless the State or Government was too poor to do so?

On the other hand, the presence of an army nearby causes prices to rise, and high prices lead to the people's wealth being drained. (Wang Hsi says that prices increase even before the army leaves its own territory. Ts'ao Kung believes this applies to an army that has already crossed the frontier.)

When the people's wealth is drained, the farmers will suffer from heavy demands placed upon them.

As their wealth is lost and their strength is exhausted, the homes of the people will be left bare, and three-tenths of their income will be consumed. (Tu Mu and Wang Hsi argue that the people are actually deprived of seven-tenths of their income, but this is difficult to extract from the text. Ho Shih adds a characteristic note: "The people are the essential part of the State, and food is their heaven, so is it not right that those in authority should take care to protect both?")

Meanwhile, government expenses for damaged chariots, worn-out horses, breastplates, helmets, bows and arrows, spears and shields, protective coverings, oxen for transportation, and heavy wagons will consume four-tenths of the total revenue.

Thus, a wise general makes it a priority to forage from the enemy. One cartload of the enemy's provisions is worth twenty of one's own, and similarly, a single picul of their supplies is worth twenty from one's own stores. (This is because twenty cartloads of provisions will be consumed during the transportation of one cartload to the front. A picul is a unit of measure equal to 133.3 pounds, or 65.5 kilograms.)

Now, to defeat the enemy, our soldiers must be stirred to anger; and to gain any benefit from defeating the enemy, they must receive rewards. (Tu Mu explains: "Rewards are necessary so the soldiers understand the benefit of beating the enemy. When spoils are captured from the enemy, they should be distributed as rewards, so that all the men will have a strong desire to fight, each for his own gain.")

Therefore, in chariot warfare, when ten or more chariots are captured, the soldiers who take the first one should be rewarded. Our flags should be substituted for the enemy's, and the captured chariots should be integrated and used alongside our own. Captured enemy soldiers should be treated kindly and kept.

This is called using the enemy's resources to strengthen one's own forces.

In war, your main objective should always be victory, not prolonged campaigns. (As Ho Shih remarks: "War is not something to be treated lightly." Sun Tzu reiterates here the central lesson of this chapter.)

Thus, it is clear that the leader of armies holds the fate of the people in his hands, and it is his actions that determine whether the nation will be at peace or in danger.

Chapter 3 - Attack By Stratagem

Sun Tzu said: In the practical art of war, the best course of action is to take the enemy's country whole and intact; to shatter and destroy it is not as good. Likewise, it is better to capture an entire army than to destroy it, better to capture an entire regiment, detachment, or company than to destroy them. (According to Ssu-ma Fa, an army corps consisted of 12,500 men; Ts'ao Kung says a regiment contained 500 men, a detachment could consist of any number between 100 and 500, and a company could range from 5 to 100 men. However, Chang Yu gives the exact figures of 100 for a detachment and 5 for a company.)

Therefore, to fight and win in all your battles is not the highest excellence; the highest excellence consists in breaking the enemy's resistance without having to fight. (Once again, no modern strategist would disagree with these words. Moltke's greatest victory, the surrender of the enormous French army at Sedan, was achieved virtually without bloodshed.)

Thus, the highest form of generalship is to thwart the enemy's plans. (Perhaps the word "thwart" does not fully capture the meaning of the original Chinese, which implies not merely defending by countering each of the enemy's strategies, but actively attacking. Ho Shih explains this clearly in his note: "When the enemy plans to attack us, we must anticipate him by launching our attack first.")

The next best course is to prevent the enemy's forces from combining. (This involves isolating him from his allies. We must remember that Sun Tzu is referring to the many states or principalities into which China was divided in his time.)

After that, the next best option is to attack the enemy's army in the field. (That is, when his forces are already gathered and at full strength.)

The worst course of action is to besiege walled cities.

The rule is not to attack cities with walls unless it is absolutely necessary.

(Another good piece of military advice. If the Boers had followed this in 1899 and not spread their forces thin around places like Kimberley, Mafeking, or even Ladysmith, they likely would have had the upper hand before the British were really ready to fight back.)

Building mantlets, movable shelters, and other war tools will take up three whole months.

(It's not completely clear what the Chinese term translated as "mantlets" really meant. Ts'ao Kung says they were "large shields," but Li Ch'uan gives us a better idea, describing them as protection for soldiers attacking the walls of a city up close. This suggests they might have been like the Roman testudo, a formation where soldiers would use their shields to form a shell. Tu Mu claims they were wheeled vehicles for defense, but Ch'en Hao disagrees. See earlier, II.14. The term also referred to turrets on city walls. The "movable shelters" were more clearly described by various commentators: they were wooden, missile-proof structures with four wheels, covered with raw hides, used in sieges to transport soldiers safely to and from the city walls, often to fill up moats with dirt. Tu Mu adds that nowadays they are called "wooden donkeys.")

Building up ramps against the walls will take another three months.

(These were large mounds or earth ramps built up to the height of the enemy's walls to spot weak points in the defenses and to tear down the fortified turrets mentioned earlier.)

The general, unable to keep his anger in check, will send his men to attack like a swarm of ants.

(This vivid image from Ts'ao Kung comes from the sight of an army of ants climbing up a wall. It means the general, losing patience due to the delay, may order an attack before his war machines are ready.)

As a result, one-third of his men will be killed, and the city will still not be taken. These are the terrible outcomes of a siege.

(We are reminded of the heavy losses suffered by the Japanese in their recent siege of Port Arthur.)

A skilled leader defeats the enemy's troops without ever having to fight; he takes their cities without needing to lay siege; he brings down their kingdom without long, drawn-out battles.

(Chia Lin points out that the leader only removes the government but does not harm individuals. A classic example of this is Wu Wang, who, after ending the Yin dynasty, was celebrated as the "Father and mother of the people.")

With his army fully intact, he will challenge for control of the Empire, and by doing so, without losing a single man, his victory will be complete.

(Because of the double meanings in the Chinese text, the second part of this sentence could also mean: "And thus, since the weapon has not been dulled by overuse, its sharpness remains perfect.")

This is how to conquer through strategy.

In war, if our forces outnumber the enemy ten to one, we surround him; if five to one, we attack him.

(Immediately, without waiting for any further advantages.)

If we are twice as numerous, we split our army into two.

(Tu Mu disagrees with this advice, and at first glance, it seems to go against a basic rule of warfare. However, Ts'ao Kung offers an explanation: "When we are two to one against the enemy, one part of our army can be used in the regular way, and the other can be used for a special maneuver." Chang Yu adds more clarity: "If our army is twice the size of the enemy's, we should split it into two groups—one to face the enemy head-on, and the other to attack from behind. If the enemy responds to the front attack, he can be crushed from behind; if he reacts to the rear attack, he can be defeated from the front." This is what is meant by saying that 'one part may be used in the regular way, and the other for a special maneuver.' Tu Mu doesn't understand that splitting the army is an irregular strategy, just as concentrating the army is the regular strategy, and he is too quick to call this a mistake.)

If we are evenly matched, we can engage in battle.

(Li Ch'uan, supported by Ho Shih, rephrases this as: "If both sides are equal in strength, only a skilled general will choose to fight.")

If we are slightly weaker, we can avoid the enemy.

(The meaning "we can watch the enemy" is an improvement on this, but there isn't much solid backing for this version. Chang Yu reminds us that this advice only holds if other factors are equal. A small difference in numbers can often be balanced out by greater energy and discipline.)

If we are greatly outmatched, we can retreat.

Even though a small force may put up a stubborn fight, in the end, it will be overcome by a larger force.

The general is the foundation of the State: if the foundation is solid in all areas, the State will be strong; if the foundation has weaknesses, the State will be weak.

(As Li Ch'uan puts it briefly: "A gap shows a weakness; if the general's ability is not perfect—if he isn't fully skilled in his role—his army will lack strength.")

There are three ways a ruler can bring disaster to his army:

(1) By ordering the army to advance or retreat without knowing that it cannot follow those orders. This is called crippling the army.

(Li Ch'uan adds: "It's like tying the legs of a racehorse so it can't run." You might think "the ruler" in this case is far away, trying to direct the army from a distance. However, the commentators interpret it the opposite way, quoting T'ai Kung: "A kingdom shouldn't be ruled from the outside, and an army shouldn't be commanded from within." Naturally, during a battle or when close to the enemy, the general shouldn't be right in the middle of his own troops, but should stay a little apart. Otherwise, he might misread the situation and give wrong orders.)

(2) By trying to govern an army in the same way he runs a kingdom, without understanding the conditions within an army, a ruler causes unrest in the soldiers' minds.

(Ts'ao Kung notes: "The military and civil spheres are entirely different; you can't handle an army with soft, delicate treatment." Chang Yu adds: "Humanity and justice are the foundations for governing a state, but not for leading an army. Opportunism and flexibility are military virtues, not civil ones.")

(3) By using officers without making distinctions between them,

(This means the ruler doesn't carefully assign the right person to the right role.) because he doesn't understand the military principle of adapting to circumstances, he undermines the soldiers' trust.(I follow Mei Yao-ch'en here. Other commentators refer to the officers employed, not the ruler as in the previous sections. Tu Yu says: "If a general doesn't understand adaptability, he should not be put in charge."

Tu Mu quotes: "A skilled leader will employ the wise, the brave, the greedy, and the foolish. The wise man enjoys proving his merit, the brave man seeks to show his courage in action, the greedy man quickly seizes opportunities, and the foolish man fears nothing, even death.")

But when the army is restless and distrustful, conflict will arise from the other feudal princes. This brings chaos into the army and throws away any chance of victory.

From this, we know that there are five key factors for victory: (1) He will win who knows when to fight and when not to fight.

(Chang Yu says: If he can fight, he moves forward and attacks; if he cannot fight, he retreats and defends. Victory is certain for the one who understands when to attack and when to defend.)

(2) He will win who knows how to manage both larger and smaller forces.

(This isn't just about the general's ability to count numbers accurately, as Li Ch'uan and others suggest. Chang Yu explains this better: "By using the art of war, a smaller force can defeat a larger one, and vice versa. The secret is understanding the terrain and seizing the right moment. As Wu Tzŭ says: 'With a larger force, move on easy ground; with a smaller force, seek difficult ground.'")

Chapter 4 - Tactical Dispositions

Ts'ao Kung explains the meaning behind the title of this chapter: "marching and countermarching by the two armies to find out each other's condition." Tu Mu adds: "It is through the positioning of an army that its state can be revealed. Hide your positioning, and your condition remains secret, leading to victory; expose your positioning, and your condition becomes clear, leading to defeat." Wang Hsi comments that a good general "ensures success by adapting his tactics to those of the enemy."

Sun Tzŭ said: The skilled fighters of the past first made sure they could not be defeated, then waited for the right moment to defeat the enemy.

The power to avoid defeat is in our own hands, but the chance to defeat the enemy comes from the enemy himself.

(That is, of course, due to a mistake on the enemy's part.)

Thus, a skilled fighter can always protect himself from defeat,

(Chang Yu explains that this is done by "concealing the positioning of the troops, covering up tracks, and taking constant precautions.") but he cannot always ensure he will defeat the enemy.Hence the saying: One may know how to win but still not be able to achieve it.

Protecting oneself from defeat involves defensive tactics, while defeating the enemy involves taking the offensive.

(I keep the meaning found in a similar passage in §§ 1-3, despite the fact that the commentators disagree with me. Their interpretation, "He who cannot conquer takes the defensive," is reasonable, but this version seems clearer.)

Being on the defensive suggests a lack of strength, while attacking shows an abundance of strength.

A general skilled in defense hides in the deepest recesses of the earth;

(Literally, "hides under the ninth earth," a metaphor for complete secrecy and concealment, so the enemy doesn't know his location.) while a general skilled in attack strikes from the highest heavens.(Another metaphor, meaning he falls upon his enemy like a sudden thunderbolt, against which there is no time to prepare. Most commentators agree with this interpretation.)

Thus, on one hand, we have the ability to protect ourselves; on the other, the ability to achieve a complete victory.

To see victory only when it is clear to everyone is not the height of excellence.

(As Ts'ao Kung says, "the key is to see the plant before it has sprouted," meaning to foresee the outcome before the action begins. Li Ch'uan mentions the story of Han Hsin, who, before attacking the much larger army of Chao, which was heavily fortified in the city of Ch'eng-an, told his officers, "Gentlemen, we are going to destroy the enemy and will meet again at dinner." His officers didn't take him seriously and gave doubtful replies. But Han Hsin had already devised a clever plan, and as he predicted, he captured the city and crushed his enemy.)

It is also not the height of excellence if you fight and win, and the whole world says, "Well done!"

(True excellence, as Tu Mu says, lies in planning secretly, moving quietly, and outsmarting the enemy's plans so that victory is achieved without a drop of blood being shed. Sun Tzŭ praises achievements that "the world's clumsy thumb and finger cannot grasp.")

Lifting an autumn hair is not a sign of great strength;

("Autumn hair" refers to the fine fur of a hare, which is softest in autumn when it starts growing back. This phrase is commonly used by Chinese writers.)

Seeing the sun and moon is not a sign of sharp vision, and hearing the sound of thunder is not a sign of quick hearing.

(Ho Shih provides examples of true strength, sharp vision, and quick hearing: Wu Huo, who could lift a 250-stone tripod; Li Chu, who could see objects as small as mustard seeds from a hundred paces; and Shih K'uang, a blind musician who could hear a mosquito's footsteps.)

What the ancients called a clever fighter is someone who not only wins, but wins with ease.

(The second part literally means "one who, while conquering, excels in conquering easily." Mei Yao-ch'en explains: "He who only notices the obvious wins his battles with difficulty; but he who sees beneath the surface wins with ease.")

For this reason, his victories bring him neither a reputation for wisdom nor credit for bravery.

(Tu Mu explains this well: "Since his victories are achieved under circumstances that remain hidden, the world at large knows nothing of them, and he gains no reputation for wisdom. Since the enemy surrenders without bloodshed, he gets no credit for bravery.")

He wins his battles by making no mistakes.

(Ch'en Hao says: "He avoids unnecessary marches and pointless attacks." Chang Yu explains the connection: "One who tries to win by brute force, even if skilled in fighting pitched battles, may sometimes be defeated. But one who can foresee the future and understand conditions before they arise will never make a mistake, and thus always win.")

Making no mistakes ensures victory because it means defeating an enemy who is already defeated.

Thus, the skilled fighter places himself in a position where defeat is impossible and never misses the moment to defeat the enemy.

(A "counsel of perfection," as Tu Mu notes. "Position" isn't just about the physical location of troops; it includes all the preparations and arrangements that a wise general makes to ensure the safety of the army.)

In war, the victorious strategist seeks battle only after victory is already assured, while the one destined for defeat fights first and then looks for victory.

(Ho Shih explains this paradox: "In warfare, first make plans that will guarantee victory, then lead your army into battle. If you rely on brute strength alone without first using strategy, victory will no longer be guaranteed.")

The ideal leader follows the moral law and adheres strictly to method and discipline; by doing so, he can control success.

In terms of military methods, there are: first, Measurement; second, Estimation of quantity; third, Calculation; fourth, Balancing of chances; and fifth, Victory.

Measurement depends on the Earth; Estimation of quantity comes from Measurement; Calculation comes from Estimation of quantity; Balancing of chances comes from Calculation; and Victory comes from Balancing of chances.

(It's hard to distinguish the four terms clearly in Chinese. The first seems to refer to surveying and measuring the ground, which allows us to estimate the enemy's strength and make calculations from that information. This leads to a weighing of chances—comparing the enemy's chances with our own. If the scale tips in our favor, victory follows. The difficulty lies in the third term, which some commentators interpret as a calculation of numbers, making it nearly synonymous with the second term. Perhaps the second refers to considering the enemy's general situation, while the third refers to estimating his numerical strength. Tu Mu suggests that once relative strength is known, we can apply cunning strategies. Ho Shih supports this, but with a weaker interpretation, indicating that the third term points to calculating numbers.)

A victorious army facing a defeated one is like a pound's weight against a single grain.

(Literally, "a victorious army is like an i (20 ounces) weighed against a shu (1/24 of an ounce); a defeated army is a shu weighed against an i." This illustrates the huge advantage a disciplined, victorious force has over one demoralized by defeat. Legge, in his note on Mencius, I.2.ix.2, defines the i as 24 Chinese ounces and corrects Chu Hsi's claim that it equals only 20 ounces. However, Li Ch'uan of the T'ang dynasty supports Chu Hsi's figure.)

The rush of a victorious force is like water bursting through a dam into a chasm a thousand fathoms deep. This concludes the section on tactical dispositions.

Chapter 5 - Energy

Sun Tzŭ said: Controlling a large army is based on the same principles as controlling a small group; it is simply a matter of dividing them into smaller units.

(This means splitting the army into regiments, companies, etc., each with its own subordinate officers. Tu Mu reminds us of the famous conversation between Han Hsin and the first Han Emperor. The Emperor asked, "How large an army do you think I could lead?" Han Hsin replied, "No more than 100,000 men, Your Majesty." "And how about you?" asked the Emperor. Han Hsin responded, "Oh, the more, the better.")

Fighting with a large army under your command is no different from fighting with a small one; it's just about using signs and signals to communicate.

To ensure that your entire force can withstand the enemy's attack without breaking, you need to use both direct and indirect maneuvers.

(Now we come to one of the most interesting parts of Sun Tzŭ's teachings: the discussion of cheng (direct) and ch'i (indirect). These two terms are tricky to fully grasp or consistently translate into English, so it's helpful to consider what various commentators have said. Li Ch'uan explains that cheng is a frontal confrontation, while ch'i is a diversion to the side. Chia Lin says: "When facing the enemy, your troops should be arranged in a conventional way, but victory comes from using unconventional maneuvers." Mei Yao-ch'en adds: "Ch'i is active, while cheng is passive; waiting for the right moment is passive, but action itself brings victory." Ho Shih explains: "We must make the enemy think our straightforward attack is secretly planned, and vice versa. Thus, cheng can become ch'i and ch'i can become cheng." He uses the example of Han Hsin, who marched his army toward Lin-chin but suddenly sent a large force across the Yellow River in wooden tubs, catching the enemy off guard. In this case, the march on Lin-chin was cheng, and the surprise maneuver across the river was ch'i."

Chang Yu summarizes these ideas by noting that military writers disagree on the definitions of cheng and ch'i. Wei Liao Tzŭ says, "Direct warfare favors frontal attacks, while indirect warfare favors attacks from behind." Ts'ao Kung says, "Going directly into battle is cheng, while appearing behind the enemy is ch'i." Li Wei-kung adds, "In war, marching straight ahead is cheng; turning movements are ch'i." These writers treat cheng and ch'i as separate and fixed, but they don't realize that the two can blend together and switch, like two sides of a circle. A comment on the T'ang Emperor T'ai Tsung goes deeper: "A ch'i maneuver becomes cheng if we make the enemy believe it is cheng; then our real attack will be ch'i, and vice versa. The secret lies in confusing the enemy so they cannot understand our true intentions."

In simpler terms, any operation is cheng if it draws the enemy's attention, and ch'i if it catches them by surprise. If the enemy recognizes a movement meant to be ch'i, it becomes cheng.)

The impact of your army should be like a grindstone smashing against an egg—this is achieved through understanding weak points and strong ones.

In all battles, the direct method may be used to engage the enemy, but indirect methods are necessary to secure victory.

(Chang Yu explains: "Develop indirect tactics steadily, either by striking at the enemy's flanks or attacking from behind." A brilliant example of indirect tactics deciding a campaign was Lord Roberts' night march around Peiwar Kotal during the second Afghan war.)

Indirect tactics, when applied efficiently, are as limitless as Heaven and Earth, as unceasing as the flow of rivers and streams. Like the sun and moon, they end only to begin again; like the four seasons, they pass and return.

(Tu Yu and Chang Yu see this as referring to the changing use of ch'i and cheng. However, Sun Tzŭ isn't specifically talking about cheng here, unless, as Cheng Yu-hsien suggests, a part of the text about cheng was lost. As mentioned before, ch'i and cheng are so interconnected in military operations that they cannot be considered separately. This passage expresses the almost endless resourcefulness of a great leader.)

There are only five musical notes, yet their combinations create more melodies than can ever be heard.

There are only five primary colors—blue, yellow, red, white, and black—yet their combinations produce more hues than can ever be seen.

There are only five basic tastes—sour, acrid, salty, sweet, and bitter—but their combinations yield more flavors than can ever be tasted.

In battle, there are only two methods of attack—the direct and the indirect—yet their combination creates an infinite number of maneuvers.

The direct and the indirect lead into each other, like a circle that has no end. Who can exhaust the possibilities of their combination?

The advance of troops is like the rush of a torrent, powerful enough to carry stones along its path.

The quality of decision is like the well-timed swoop of a falcon that enables it to strike and destroy its target.

(The Chinese here is tricky, and a certain key word in this context resists the best efforts of translation. Tu Mu defines this word as "the measurement or estimation of distance." But applying this meaning to the falcon, it seems to refer to the instinct of self-restraint, which prevents the bird from swooping down on its prey until the right moment, along with the ability to judge when that moment has come. The analogous quality in soldiers is the important skill of holding back their fire until the exact moment when it will be most effective. When the Victory went into action at Trafalgar, moving at hardly more than a drifting pace, it was under heavy fire for several minutes without returning a single shot. Nelson waited coolly until he was in close range, at which point the broadside he unleashed inflicted devastating damage on the enemy's nearest ships.)

Therefore, the skilled fighter will be fearsome in his attack and prompt in his decision.

(The word "decision" likely refers to the measurement of distance mentioned earlier, holding off until the enemy is close enough to strike. However, I also believe that Sun Tzŭ meant this word figuratively, similar to our own expression "short and sharp." Wang Hsi's note expands on the falcon's method of attack, adding: "This is how the 'psychological moment' should be seized in war.")

Energy may be compared to the bending of a crossbow; decision, to the release of the trigger.

(None of the commentators seem to grasp the true meaning of this simile. The key point is that energy, like the force stored in a bent crossbow, only becomes effective when released by the decision to pull the trigger.)

Amid the turmoil and chaos of battle, there may seem to be disorder, yet there is no real disorder; amid confusion, your formation may appear to lack head or tail, yet it remains unshakable against defeat.

(Mei Yao-ch'en says: "When the subdivisions of the army have been arranged in advance, and the various signals have been agreed upon, the separating, joining, dispersing, and regrouping that occurs during battle may give the appearance of disorder, but true disorder is impossible. Even if your formation seems headless and without direction, your forces will not be routed.")

Simulated disorder requires perfect discipline; simulated fear requires courage; simulated weakness requires strength.

(To make this translation clearer, the sharp paradox of the original needs to be softened. Ts'ao Kung hints at the meaning in his brief note: "These things are all meant to disrupt the enemy's formation and conceal one's true condition." Tu Mu explains it plainly: "If you want to appear confused to lure the enemy, you must first have perfect discipline; if you want to display fear to trap the enemy, you must have great courage; if you want to show weakness to make the enemy overconfident, you must have great strength.")

Hiding order beneath the appearance of disorder is simply a matter of dividing the army into smaller units.

(See earlier, § 1.)

Concealing courage under a display of timidity requires a reservoir of hidden energy.

(The commentators interpret a specific Chinese word here differently than elsewhere in the chapter. Tu Mu says: "When the enemy sees that we are in a favorable position but make no move, they will believe we are truly afraid.")

Masking strength with weakness is accomplished through strategic positioning.

(Chang Yu recounts the story of Kao Tsu, the first Han Emperor. He wanted to attack the Hsiung-nu, so he sent spies to gather intelligence on their condition. However, the Hsiung-nu, anticipating this, hid all their strong soldiers and healthy horses, and only allowed the spies to see old soldiers and weak animals. As a result, all the spies advised the Emperor to attack. Only Lou Ching opposed them, saying: "When two countries prepare for war, they naturally try to show their strength. Since our spies have only seen old and weak forces, this must be a trick, and attacking would be unwise." The Emperor ignored this advice, fell into the trap, and was surrounded at Po-teng.)

Thus, one who is skilled at keeping the enemy on the move uses deceptive appearances, to which the enemy will respond.

(Ts'ao Kung notes: "Create the appearance of weakness and need." Tu Mu adds: "If our forces are stronger than the enemy's, we can pretend to be weak to lure them in; but if we are weaker, we must make the enemy believe we are strong so they stay away. In fact, the enemy's actions should always be based on the signals we choose to give." There is an anecdote about Sun Pin, a descendant of Sun Wu: In 341 B.C., the state of Ch'i was at war with Wei, and Sun Pin was sent to face the general P'ang Chuan, who was his personal enemy. Sun Pin said: "The Ch'i state is known for cowardice, so our enemy will underestimate us. Let's take advantage of this." When their army crossed into Wei territory, Sun Pin ordered 100,000 campfires on the first night, 50,000 on the second night, and only 20,000 on the third night. P'ang Chuan, in pursuit, thought: "I knew these Ch'i soldiers were cowards; their numbers are already less than half." Sun Pin retreated to a narrow pass, knowing that P'ang Chuan would arrive after dark. There, Sun Pin had a tree stripped of its bark and inscribed: "Under this tree, P'ang Chuan will die." As night fell, Sun Pin hid archers nearby, instructing them to shoot when they saw light. When P'ang Chuan arrived, he struck a light to read the inscription on the tree, and was immediately shot down by arrows, throwing his army into confusion. [Tu Mu's version of the story is more dramatic, though the Shih Chi suggests that after the defeat of his army, P'ang Chuan committed suicide in despair.])

He sacrifices something, knowing the enemy will snatch at it.

By offering baits, he keeps the enemy on the move; then, with a group of carefully chosen men, he waits to ambush him.

(With an adjustment suggested by Li Ching, this reads: "He lies in wait with the main body of his troops.")

The clever combatant relies on the effect of combined energy and does not demand too much from individuals.

(Tu Mu explains: "First, he assesses the overall power of his army as a whole; then he takes individual abilities into account and uses each person according to their talents. He does not expect perfection from those who lack it.")

This is why he can select the right men and make use of their combined strength.

When he employs combined energy, his fighters become like rolling logs or stones. A log or stone remains still on level ground but moves when placed on a slope. If it is square, it stops, but if it is round, it rolls down.

(Ts'ao Kung refers to this as "the use of natural or inherent power.")

Thus, the energy generated by skilled fighters is like the momentum of a round stone rolling down a mountain thousands of feet high. This concludes the discussion on energy.

(Tu Mu points out that the main lesson of this chapter is the critical importance of rapid maneuvers and sudden charges in warfare. "With such tactics," he adds, "great results can be achieved with even small forces.")

Chapter 6 – Weak Points and Strong

[Chang Yu tries to explain the sequence of the chapters in this way: "Chapter IV, on Tactical Dispositions, dealt with offense and defense; Chapter V, on Energy, covered direct and indirect methods. The skilled general first familiarizes himself with the theory of attack and defense, and then focuses on direct and indirect methods. He learns how to vary and combine these two methods before moving on to the topic of weak and strong points. The use of direct or indirect methods arises from attack and defense, and recognizing weak and strong points depends on understanding these methods. Therefore, this chapter follows directly after the one on Energy."]

Sun Tzŭ said: Whoever is first to arrive on the battlefield and waits for the enemy will be well-prepared for the fight; whoever arrives second and has to rush into battle will be tired and worn out.

Therefore, the clever combatant imposes his will on the enemy and never allows the enemy to impose his will on him.

(A mark of a great soldier is that he fights on his own terms or not at all.)

By offering advantages, he can lure the enemy to approach; or by causing harm, he can prevent the enemy from drawing near.

(In the first case, he entices with bait; in the second, he strikes a key point the enemy will be forced to defend.)

If the enemy is resting, he can harass him;

(This passage can be cited as evidence against Mei Yao-ch'en's interpretation of I. § 23.) if the enemy has plenty of food, he can starve him out; if the enemy is quietly encamped, he can force him to move.Appear at points the enemy must rush to defend; march quickly to places where you are not expected.

An army can cover great distances without suffering if it travels through areas where the enemy is absent.

(Ts'ao Kung summarizes this well: "Emerge from the void—like a surprise attack—and strike at vulnerable spots, avoid defended places, and attack where you are least expected.")

You can be certain of success in your attacks if you only strike at places that are undefended.

(Wang Hsi explains "undefended places" as weak points, meaning areas where the general is lacking in ability, the soldiers lack morale, the walls are not strong enough, precautions are too lax, reinforcements arrive too late, supplies are insufficient, or the defenders are in conflict among themselves.)

You can ensure the safety of your defense if you

only hold positions that cannot be attacked.

(That is, where none of the weaknesses mentioned above exist. There's an interesting nuance in interpreting this line. Tu Mu, Ch'en Hao, and Mei Yao-ch'en suggest it means: "To make your defense completely secure, you must even defend places that are unlikely to be attacked," and Tu Mu adds, "How much more so for places that are likely to be attacked." However, this interpretation doesn't balance well with the preceding clause, which is important in the highly antithetical style typical of Chinese writing. Chang Yu seems closer to the point by saying: "The skilled attacker strikes from the topmost heights of heaven [see IV. § 7], making it impossible for the enemy to defend. Thus, the places I will attack are exactly those the enemy cannot defend. The skilled defender hides in the deepest recesses of the earth, making it impossible for the enemy to locate him. Thus, the places I will hold are precisely those the enemy cannot attack.")

Therefore, the general who is skilled in attack confuses the enemy, so they do not know what to defend; the general who is skilled in defense confounds the enemy, so they do not know what to attack.

(An aphorism that sums up the essence of the art of war.)

O divine art of subtlety and secrecy! Through you, we learn to be invisible, through you, we learn to be inaudible;

(Literally, "without form or sound," in reference to the enemy.) and thus, we hold the enemy's fate in our hands. You can advance and be absolutely unstoppable if you strike at the enemy's weak points; you can retreat safely and avoid pursuit if your movements are quicker than the enemy's.

If we want to engage in battle, we can force the enemy to fight, even if he is hiding behind a high wall and a deep trench. All we need to do is attack another place that he will be forced to defend.

(Tu Mu explains: "If the enemy is the invader, we can cut off his supply lines and seize the roads he must use to retreat; if we are the invaders, we can aim our attack at the ruler himself." It's clear that Sun Tzŭ, unlike certain generals in later conflicts such as the Boer War, did not believe in frontal assaults.)

If we do not wish to fight, we can prevent the enemy from engaging us, even if our encampment is only outlined on the ground. All we need to do is confuse him with something strange and unexpected.

(This concise phrase is paraphrased by Chia Lin as: "even though we have constructed neither walls nor ditches." Li Ch'uan adds: "we bewilder him with strange and unusual tactics," and Tu Mu illustrates with three anecdotes. One example is Chu-ko Liang, who, when stationed at Yang-p'ing and about to be attacked by Ssu-ma I, unexpectedly struck his flags, silenced his drums, and opened the city gates, showing only a few men sweeping the grounds. This strange move made Ssu-ma I suspect a trap, causing him to withdraw his army. What Sun Tzŭ is advocating here, therefore, is nothing less than the skillful use of "bluff.")

By discovering the enemy's plans while keeping our own concealed, we can concentrate our forces, while the enemy is forced to divide his.

(The conclusion may not seem obvious at first, but Chang Yu, following Mei Yao-ch'en, explains: "If the enemy's plans are visible, we can attack him with a united force; meanwhile, if our plans are kept secret, the enemy will have to split his forces to guard against attacks from multiple directions.")

We can form a single, united force, while the enemy must divide into smaller parts. Thus, we will have a whole army against only fragments of the enemy's force, meaning we will be many against their few.

If we are able to attack an inferior force with a superior one in this way, the enemy will find themselves in great difficulty.

The location where we intend to fight must not be revealed, because this will force the enemy to prepare for possible attacks at several different points.

(Sheridan once explained General Grant's victories by saying that "while his opponents were kept fully occupied wondering what he was going to do, he was focused mainly on what he was going to do.")

With the enemy's forces scattered in many directions, the number of troops we face at any given point will be relatively small.

For if the enemy strengthens his front lines, he will weaken his rear; if he strengthens his rear, he will weaken his front. If he strengthens his left, he will weaken his right, and if he strengthens his right, he will weaken his left. If he sends reinforcements everywhere, he will be weak everywhere.

(Frederick the Great, in his Instructions to his Generals, wrote: "A defensive war tends to lead us into making too many detachments. Generals with little experience try to defend every point, while those who understand their profession focus only on the main objective, allowing small losses to avoid greater ones.")

Numerical weakness arises from having to prepare against possible attacks, while numerical strength comes from forcing the enemy to make such preparations.

(Colonel Henderson described the highest form of generalship as "compelling the enemy to disperse his army, then concentrating a superior force against each fraction in turn.")

If we know the place and time of the coming battle, we can gather our forces from even the greatest distances to fight.

(Sun Tzŭ is referring to the careful calculation of distances and the expert use of strategy that allow a general to divide his army for a long and rapid march, then bring them together at precisely the right place and time to confront the enemy with overwhelming strength. A dramatic example of this in military history is the appearance of Blücher at the critical moment during the Battle of Waterloo.)

But if neither the time nor place of battle is known, then the left wing will be powerless to help the right, the right will be equally unable to help the left, the front will not be able to relieve the rear, and the rear won't be able to support the front. This is even more true if the furthest parts of the army are separated by over a hundred li and the nearest by several li.

(The Chinese text here lacks precision, but the idea is likely that of an army advancing toward a rendezvous in separate columns, each with orders to meet on a specific date. If the general lets the detachments march haphazardly without precise instructions on when and where to meet, the enemy could destroy the army piece by piece. Chang Yu's note clarifies: "If we do not know the enemy's concentration point or the day they plan to engage, our unity will be lost as we prepare for defense, and the positions we hold will be insecure. If we suddenly encounter a strong enemy, we will be forced into battle in a disorganized state, with no mutual support between wings, vanguard, or rear, especially if there is a great distance between the leading and rear divisions of the army.")

Even though, by my estimation, the soldiers of Yüeh outnumber us, that will not give them any advantage in achieving victory. I say, then, that victory can be achieved.

(Unfortunately, this confident claim was not borne out. The long-standing feud between Wu and Yüeh ended in 473 B.C. with the complete defeat of Wu by Kou Chien, and Wu was absorbed into Yüeh. This likely occurred long after Sun Tzŭ's death. Chang Yu is the only commentator to note the apparent contradiction here, which he explains: "In the chapter on Tactical Dispositions, it is said, 'One may know how to conquer without being able to do it,' whereas here, it says that victory can be achieved. The difference is that in the former chapter, discussing offense and defense, it is acknowledged that if the enemy is fully prepared, victory is not guaranteed. But this passage refers specifically to the soldiers of Yüeh, who, according to Sun Tzŭ's calculations, would remain unaware of the time and place of the impending battle. That's why he says here that victory is possible.")

Though the enemy may have greater numbers, we can prevent him from engaging in battle. Devise schemes to uncover his plans and assess the likelihood of their success.

(An alternate reading offered by Chia Lin is: "Know beforehand all strategies that will lead to our success and the enemy's failure.")

Provoke him, and observe the principle behind his activity or inactivity.

(Chang Yu explains that by noting the enemy's emotional reactions—whether joy or anger—when disturbed, we can deduce whether his strategy is to remain passive or take action. He gives the example of Cho-ku Liang, who sent a woman's head-dress as an insulting gift to Ssu-ma I, provoking him to abandon his cautious, passive tactics.)

Force the enemy to reveal himself, so you can discover his weak points.

Carefully compare the enemy's army with your own, so you will know where strength is abundant and where it is lacking.

(See also IV. § 6.)

In making tactical plans, the highest achievement is to keep them hidden.

(The paradox loses some sharpness in translation. Concealment here doesn't necessarily mean literal invisibility (see § 9 above), but rather not showing any signs of what you intend to do—keeping your thoughts and plans completely veiled.)

Hide your dispositions, and you will be protected from the prying eyes of even the most clever spies and the schemes of the wisest minds.

(Tu Mu explains: "Even if the enemy has intelligent and capable officers, they will not be able to make any effective plans against us.")

How victory is brought about using the enemy's own tactics is something the masses cannot understand.

Everyone can see the tactics by which I win, but no one can see the strategy behind that victory.

(That is, people can observe the outward methods used in winning a battle, but they cannot see the long process of planning and the combinations of strategies that precede it.)

Do not simply repeat the tactics that won you a previous victory; instead, let your methods be shaped by the infinite variety of circumstances.

(Wang Hsi wisely notes: "There is only one core principle of victory, but the tactics leading to it are countless." Compare this to Colonel Henderson's view: "The rules of strategy are few and simple, and can be learned in a week. However, knowing them will not teach a person to lead an army like Napoleon any more than knowing grammar will teach someone to write like Gibbon.")

Military tactics are like water; for just as water flows away from high ground and moves quickly downhill, so in war, the way is to avoid the strong and strike at the weak.(Like water, which follows the path of least resistance.)

Water shapes its course according to the nature of the ground over which it flows; in the same way, a soldier works out his victory in relation to the enemy he is facing.

Therefore, just as water has no constant shape, so there are no constant conditions in warfare.

He who can adjust his tactics to match the situation and succeed in winning may be called a captain born of heaven.

The five elements (water, fire, wood, metal, earth) are not always equally dominant;

(Wang Hsi notes: "They dominate in turn.")

The four seasons give way to each other in succession.

(Literally, "they do not always remain in the same place.")

There are short days and long days; the moon waxes and wanes.

(See also V. § 6. The point here is to illustrate the ever-changing nature of war by comparing it to the constant shifts in nature. The comparison is not entirely perfect, however, since the regularity of natural phenomena differs from the unpredictability of war.)

Chapter 7 - Manoeuvering

Sun Tzŭ said: In war, the general receives his orders from the sovereign.

After gathering an army and concentrating his forces, he must blend and harmonize the various elements within it before setting up camp.

(Chang Yu explains: "This refers to creating harmony and trust between the higher and lower ranks before going to battle." He also quotes Wu Tzŭ: "Without harmony in the State, no military campaign can be undertaken; without harmony in the army, no battle formation can be made." In a historical romance, Sun Tzŭ is portrayed telling Wu Yuan: "In general, those who wage war must resolve all internal issues before attacking an external enemy.")

After that comes tactical maneuvering, which is more difficult than anything else.

(I've slightly adjusted the traditional interpretation of Ts'ao Kung, who says: "From the time we receive the sovereign's instructions until we set up camp opposite the enemy, the tactics are the most challenging." It seems more accurate to say that tactics and maneuvers truly begin after the army has marched out and encamped. Ch'ien Hao's note supports this view: "For recruiting, concentrating, harmonizing, and fortifying an army, there are many established rules. The real challenge comes when we start tactical operations." Tu Yu also remarks that "the greatest difficulty is in seizing favorable positions before the enemy does.")

The difficulty of tactical maneuvering lies in turning the indirect into the direct, and transforming misfortune into advantage.

(This sentence is one of Sun Tzŭ's typically condensed and somewhat cryptic expressions. Ts'ao Kung explains: "Make it seem as though you are far away, then cover the distance quickly and arrive before your opponent." Tu Mu says: "Deceive the enemy so that he becomes relaxed and slow while you advance with utmost speed." Ho Shih offers another perspective: "Even if you have difficult terrain to cross or natural obstacles in your way, this disadvantage can be turned into an advantage through rapid movement." Famous examples include Hannibal's crossing of the Alps, which put Italy at his mercy, and Napoleon's similar feat two thousand years later, resulting in the victory at Marengo.)

Thus, taking a long and circuitous route, while luring the enemy out of position, and although starting later than him, managing to reach the goal before him, demonstrates skill in the art of deviation.

(Tu Mu references the famous march of Chao She in 270 B.C. to relieve the town of O-yu, which was under siege by a Ch'in army. The King of Chao initially sought advice from Lien P'o, who considered the distance too far and the terrain too difficult for a relief mission. However, Chao She, acknowledging the risk, boldly stated: "We will be like two rats fighting in a hole—the braver one will win!" After setting out with his army, Chao She marched only 30 li before stopping to build fortifications for 28 days, ensuring the enemy's spies would report this delay. The Ch'in general, thinking Chao She was unwilling to save a city outside Chao's direct control, relaxed. But as soon as the spies left, Chao She launched a forced march, covering two days and one night, and arrived so swiftly that he seized the advantageous North hill before the enemy knew of his movements. The result was a decisive defeat for the Ch'in, forcing them to abandon the siege and retreat.)

Maneuvering with a disciplined army is advantageous; with an undisciplined multitude, it is most dangerous.

(I adopt the reading of the T'ung Tien, Cheng Yu-hsien, and the T'u Shu for clarity. The commentators using the standard text suggest that maneuvering can be either profitable or dangerous, depending on the general's skill.)

If you march a fully equipped army to seize an advantage, chances are you will be too late. However, sending a flying column for the task often requires sacrificing baggage and supplies.

(Some of the Chinese text is unclear even to the commentators, who paraphrase it. I offer my own translation cautiously, as there seems to be some deeper corruption in the text. Nonetheless, it is apparent that Sun Tzŭ disapproves of undertaking a long march without proper supplies. See § 11 below.)

If you order your soldiers to roll up their coats and make forced marches without stopping day or night, covering twice the usual distance in one go, traveling a hundred li to gain an advantage, the leaders of all your three divisions will end up in the hands of the enemy.

The strongest men will be at the front, while the exhausted ones will fall behind, and following this plan, only one-tenth of your army will reach the destination.

The moral of this, as Ts'ao Kung and others have pointed out, is that you should not march a hundred li to gain a tactical advantage, whether with or without your baggage train. Maneuvers like this should be limited to shorter distances. Stonewall Jackson said: "The hardships of forced marches are often more painful than the dangers of battle." He rarely asked his troops for extraordinary efforts. It was only when he planned a surprise attack or when a rapid retreat was urgently needed that he sacrificed everything for speed.

If you march fifty li to outmaneuver the enemy, the leader of your first division will be lost, and only half of your army will reach the goal.

If you march thirty li for the same purpose, two-thirds of your army will arrive.

From this, we can understand how difficult tactical maneuvers can be.

An army without its baggage train is lost; without provisions, it is lost; without supply bases, it is lost.

I think Sun Tzŭ meant "stores accumulated in depots." But Tu Yu says "fodder and the like," Chang Yu says "goods in general," and Wang Hsi says "fuel, salt, foodstuffs, etc."

We cannot form alliances until we understand the plans of our neighbors.

We are not fit to lead an army on the march unless we are familiar with the terrain—its mountains and forests, its pitfalls and cliffs, its marshes and swamps.

We will not be able to take advantage of natural terrain unless we make use of local guides.

In war, practice deception, and you will succeed. In the tactics of Turenne, deceiving the enemy, especially about the number of his troops, played a very important role.

Only move when there is a real advantage to be gained.

Whether to concentrate or divide your troops must be determined by the circumstances.

Let your speed be as swift as the wind,

(The simile is especially fitting because the wind is not only fast but, as Mei Yao-ch'en notes, "invisible and leaves no trace behind.") and your formations as dense as a forest.(Meng Shih's comment comes closer to the meaning: "When marching slowly, order and ranks must be preserved" to guard against surprise attacks. Natural forests don't grow in rows, but they do have the quality of compactness and density.)

When raiding and plundering, be like a raging fire,

(Compare with the Shih Ching: "Fierce as a blazing fire that no one can stop.") and when holding your position, be as immovable as a mountain.(This applies when defending a position from which the enemy tries to dislodge you or, as Tu Yu suggests, when the enemy is trying to lure you into a trap.)

Let your plans be as dark and impenetrable as night, and when you strike, hit like a thunderbolt.

(Tu Yu quotes a proverb from T'ai Kung: "You cannot close your ears to thunder or your eyes to lightning—they are too fast." Similarly, an attack should be so swift that it cannot be countered.)

When plundering the countryside, divide the spoils among your men,

(Sun Tzŭ aims to curb the abuses of indiscriminate looting by ensuring that all booty is placed in a common stock and fairly distributed among the troops.) and when you capture new territory, divide it into allotments for the soldiers.(Ch'en Hao advises: "Quarter your soldiers on the land and let them sow and cultivate it." By following this principle, harvesting the land they invaded, the Chinese succeeded in carrying out some of their most memorable expeditions, such as Pan Ch'ao's march to the Caspian, and, in more recent times, the campaigns of Fu-k'ang-an and Tso Tsung-t'ang.)

Think carefully and plan before taking any action.

(Chang Yu quotes Wei Liao Tzŭ, saying that we should not leave our camp until we understand the enemy's strength and the intelligence of their general. See the "seven comparisons" mentioned earlier.)

The one who masters the art of deception will win.

(Refer to previous sections for more on this.)

This is the essence of maneuvering.

(These words would naturally end the section, but what follows is an excerpt from an older book on war, which no longer exists but was still known during Sun Tzŭ's time. The style of the passage isn't noticeably different from Sun Tzŭ's own writing, and no commentators question its authenticity.)

The Book of Army Management says:

(It's worth noting that earlier commentators don't provide much information about this book. Mei Yao-ch'en calls it "an ancient military classic," and Wang Hsi refers to it as "an old book on war." Considering the centuries of warfare between different kingdoms in China before Sun Tzŭ's time, it's likely that military wisdom had already been written down in earlier times.)

On the battlefield,

(This is implied but not directly stated in the text.) spoken commands don't carry far enough, so gongs and drums were introduced. Similarly, normal objects can't be seen clearly in the chaos, which is why banners and flags are used.Gongs and drums, banners and flags, are used to focus the ears and eyes of the army on a single point.

(Chang Yu explains: "When sight and hearing are concentrated on the same object, the movements of as many as a million soldiers will be as coordinated as those of a single man.")

When the army forms a united body, it becomes impossible for the brave to advance alone or for the cowardly to retreat alone.

(Chuang Yu quotes: "Equally guilty are those who advance without orders and those who retreat without orders." Tu Mu tells a story of Wu Ch'i, who was fighting the Ch'in State. Before the battle began, one of his soldiers, renowned for his daring, went out on his own, captured two enemy heads, and returned to camp. Wu Ch'i had the man executed immediately. When an officer protested, saying, "This man was a good soldier and shouldn't have been beheaded," Wu Ch'i replied, "I know he was a good soldier, but I had him executed because he acted without orders.")

This is the art of managing large masses of men.

In night fighting, use signal fires and drums, and in daytime battles, use flags and banners to influence the ears and eyes of your soldiers.

(Ch'en Hao mentions Li Kuang-pi's night march to Ho-yang with 500 mounted men. They made such an impressive display with torches that the rebel leader Shih Ssu-ming, despite having a large army, didn't dare oppose their passage.)

An entire army can be robbed of its spirit.

(Chang Yu says: "In war, if a spirit of anger can fill the entire army at once, its attack will be unstoppable. The enemy's soldiers will be most eager when they first arrive, so we should not fight right away. Instead, we should wait until their enthusiasm fades before striking. This is how their spirit can be taken from them." Li Ch'uan and others tell a story from the Tso Chuan about Ts'ao Kuei, an advisor to Duke Chuang of Lu. When Lu was attacked by Ch'i, the duke prepared to fight at Ch'ang-cho after hearing the enemy's first drumbeat. Ts'ao said, "Not yet." Only after the enemy's drums sounded a third time did he give the order to attack. The army of Ch'i was defeated. When asked why he delayed, Ts'ao Kuei explained: "In battle, a courageous spirit is everything. The first drumbeat raises this spirit, but with the second it weakens, and by the third it's gone. I attacked when their spirit was gone and ours was at its peak." Wu Tzŭ lists "spirit" as the first of the "four important influences" in war, adding, "The value of an entire army—a mighty host of a million men—depends on one person: such is the power of spirit!")

A commander-in-chief can also lose his presence of mind.

(Chang Yu notes: "Presence of mind is the most vital quality for a general. It enables him to restore order from chaos and give courage to those who are panicking." The great general Li Ching once said, "Attacking does not simply mean assaulting walled cities or striking an army in battle. It also involves shaking the enemy's mental balance.")

A soldier's spirit is at its highest in the morning,

(As long as he has had breakfast, I suppose. At the Battle of the Trebia, the Romans made the mistake of fighting on an empty stomach, while Hannibal's men ate at their leisure. See Livy, XXI, liv. 8, lv. 1 and 8.) by noon, it starts to fade; and by evening, his only thought is to return to camp.A wise general, therefore, avoids fighting an army when its spirit is high, but attacks when it is sluggish and ready to retreat. This is the art of studying moods.

To remain disciplined and calm while waiting for disorder and confusion to arise among the enemy: this is the art of maintaining self-possession.

To be close to the goal while the enemy is still far, to wait in comfort while the enemy struggles, to be well-fed while the enemy is hungry: this is the art of conserving strength.

To refrain from attacking an enemy whose banners are in perfect order, or from engaging an army that is calm and confident: this is the art of understanding circumstances.

It is a basic military principle not to advance uphill against the enemy, nor to confront him when he is descending.

Do not chase an enemy who pretends to flee; do not engage soldiers whose spirits are high.

Do not take a bait offered by the enemy.

(Li Ch'uan and Tu Mu, showing a surprising lack of insight, take this literally as food or drink that might be poisoned by the enemy. Ch'en Hao and Chang Yu point out that the saying applies more broadly.)

Do not obstruct an army that is returning home.

(The commentators explain that a soldier whose heart is set on returning home will fight with extreme determination against anyone who tries to stop him, making him too dangerous to oppose. Chang Yu quotes Han Hsin: "Unbeatable is the soldier who desires nothing but to return home." A remarkable story is told of Ts'ao Ts'ao's resourcefulness in San Kuo Chi, chapter 1. In 198 A.D., Ts'ao was besieging Chang Hsiu in Jang, when Liu Piao sent reinforcements to cut off his retreat. Ts'ao was forced to withdraw but found himself trapped between two enemies guarding each exit of a narrow pass. In this desperate situation, he waited until nightfall, dug a tunnel into the mountainside, and set an ambush. Once the entire enemy army had passed, Ts'ao's hidden troops attacked from behind, while he turned to confront them from the front, throwing them into chaos and defeating them. Ts'ao later remarked, "The bandits tried to stop my retreat and forced me into a desperate fight; that's how I knew how to defeat them.")

When you surround an army, leave an opening for escape.

(This doesn't mean you should let the enemy flee. The purpose, as Tu Mu explains, is to make the enemy believe there is a way to escape, preventing them from fighting with the desperation of those with no hope. As Tu Mu adds, "Once they believe they have a way out, you can then crush them.")

Do not press a desperate enemy too hard.

(Ch'en Hao cites the saying: "When birds and beasts are cornered, they will use their claws and teeth." Chang Yu advises: "If your enemy has burned his boats and destroyed his cooking pots, fully committed to the outcome of the battle, you must not push them to the extreme." Ho Shih illustrates this with a story about the general Fu Yen-ch'ing. In 945 A.D., he and his colleague Tu Chung-wei were surrounded by a much larger Khitan army in a barren, desert-like area. Their small Chinese force was suffering due to a lack of water. The wells they dug ran dry, and the soldiers were reduced to squeezing moisture from lumps of mud. Their numbers dwindled rapidly, and Fu Yen-ch'ing declared, "We are desperate men. It is better to die for our country than to be taken captive with our hands tied." A strong wind was blowing from the northeast, filling the air with dense clouds of sand. Tu Chung-wei wanted to wait for the storm to pass before launching their final attack, but another officer, Li Shou-cheng, saw an opportunity and said, "They are many, and we are few, but in this sandstorm, our numbers won't be clear. Victory will go to those who fight hardest, and the wind will be our ally." Fu Yen-ch'ing then led a sudden and unexpected cavalry charge, routing the barbarians and breaking through to safety.)

Chapter 8 - Variation of Tactics

The heading literally means "The Nine Variations," but since Sun Tzŭ doesn't enumerate them specifically and has already stated (V §§ 6-11) that deviations in strategy are practically limitless, we are inclined to agree with Wang Hsi, who explains that "Nine" represents an indefinitely large number. It simply means that in warfare, tactics should be varied to the greatest extent possible. I am unsure how Ts'ao Kung interprets these Nine Variations, but it's suggested they are related to the Nine Situations discussed in chapter XI. This view is also supported by Chang Yu. Another possibility is that something has been lost, which is suggested by the unusual brevity of the chapter.

Sun Tzŭ said: In war, the general receives his commands from the sovereign, assembles his army, and concentrates his forces.

(This is repeated from VII. § 1, where it fits better. It may have been included here simply to provide a start for the chapter.)

When in difficult terrain, do not set up camp. In areas where main roads intersect, join hands with your allies. Do not remain in dangerously isolated positions.

(This situation is not one of the Nine Situations listed in the beginning of chapter XI, but it does appear later on (§ 43). Chang Yu defines it as being located across the border in enemy territory. Li Ch'uan says it refers to land where there are no springs, wells, flocks, or firewood. Chia Lin describes it as a region of gorges, cliffs, and steep terrain with no clear roads forward.)

In situations where you are trapped, rely on strategy. In a desperate position, you must fight.

There are roads that should not be followed,

(Li Ch'uan says this applies especially to narrow passes where ambushes are likely.) armies that must not be attacked,(It might be more accurate to say "there are times when an army should not be attacked." Ch'en Hao explains: "When you have an opportunity for a small advantage but cannot achieve a decisive victory, it is better not to attack, to avoid exhausting your troops.") towns that should not be besieged,(Compare III. § 4. Ts'ao Kung shares an example from his own experience. While invading Hsu-chou, he bypassed the city of Hua-pi, which lay in his path, and advanced deeper into the country. This strategy paid off with the capture of fourteen key cities. Chang Yu advises: "Do not attack a town that, even if captured, cannot be held or, if left alone, will not pose a threat." Hsun Ying, when urged to attack Pi-yang, responded: "The city is small and well-fortified; even if I succeed in taking it, it won't be a great achievement, but if I fail, I will be ridiculed." Sieges made up a significant part of warfare in the seventeenth century, but Turenne emphasized the value of marches, countermarches, and maneuvers. He remarked, "It is a great error to waste soldiers on capturing a town when the same effort could win an entire province.") positions that should not be contested, and commands from the sovereign that should not be obeyed.(This is difficult for the Chinese, given their strong respect for authority. Wei Liao Tzŭ, as quoted by Tu Mu, states: "Weapons are instruments of evil, conflict opposes virtue, and a military commander stands against civil order." Nonetheless, the reality remains that even the emperor's wishes must yield to military necessity.)

The general who thoroughly understands the advantages that come from varying tactics knows how to manage his troops.

The general who does not grasp these advantages, even if he is well aware of the terrain, will not be able to make effective use of his knowledge.

(Literally, “to get the advantage of the ground,” meaning not only securing favorable positions but also making the most of natural advantages in every way possible. Chang Yu explains: “Every kind of terrain has its own natural features and also offers room for variation in plans. How can these natural features be used to their full potential unless topographical knowledge is combined with a flexible mind?”)

Thus, a student of war who has not mastered the art of varying his strategies, even if he knows the Five Advantages, will fail to make the best use of his soldiers.

(Chia Lin explains that these Five Advantages refer to obvious and generally beneficial courses of action, such as: “if a road is short, it should be taken; if an army is isolated, it should be attacked; if a town is in a precarious state, it should be besieged; if a position can be stormed, it should be attempted; and if consistent with military operations, the ruler’s orders should be obeyed.” However, there are circumstances in which these advantages may not be used. For instance, “a certain road may be the shortest route, but if it is filled with natural obstacles or if the enemy has laid an ambush there, it should not be followed. A hostile force may be vulnerable to attack, but if it is desperate and ready to fight to the last, it is better not to strike.")

Therefore, in the wise leader's plans, considerations of both advantage and disadvantage are combined.

("Whether in an advantageous or disadvantageous situation," says Ts'ao Kung, "the opposite state should always be kept in mind.")

If we balance our expectation of advantage with awareness of possible disadvantages, we may successfully accomplish the most important part of our plans.

(Tu Mu comments: "If we want to gain an advantage over the enemy, we must not focus only on that goal. We must also consider the possibility of the enemy inflicting harm on us and include that in our calculations.")

If, on the other hand, we are always ready to seize an advantage even in difficult situations, we can free ourselves from misfortune.

(Tu Mu explains: "If I want to escape from a dangerous position, I must not only consider the enemy's ability to harm me but also my own ability to gain an advantage over them. If my plans balance both considerations, I will succeed in getting out of danger. For example, if I am surrounded by the enemy and only focus on escaping, the weakness of my strategy will encourage the enemy to pursue and crush me. It would be much better to encourage my troops to launch a bold counterattack and use the advantage gained to break free from the enemy's grasp." See the story of Ts'ao Ts'ao in VII. § 35, note.)

Reduce the enemy's leaders by causing harm to them.

(Chia Lin lists several ways to harm the enemy, some of which are quite unique: "Entice away the enemy's best and wisest men, leaving him without good advisors. Plant traitors in his country to disrupt government policies. Stir up intrigue and deceit, sowing discord between the ruler and his ministers. Use cunning tricks to weaken his men and drain his resources. Corrupt his morals with insidious gifts that lead him into indulgence. Unsettle his mind by presenting him with beautiful women." Chang Yu, following Wang Hsi, offers a different interpretation: "Force the enemy into a position where he is bound to suffer harm, and he will eventually submit on his own.")

Create difficulties for them,

(Tu Mu explains that this phrase means to create problems that affect the enemy's "assets"—things like a large army, a rich treasury, harmony among soldiers, and the consistent execution of orders. These are what give us leverage over the enemy.) and keep them constantly occupied.(Literally, "make servants of them." Tu Yu says: "Deny them any opportunity to rest.")

Offer deceptive attractions and lure them into rushing to a specific point.

(Meng Shih provides a great example of this idiom: "Make them forget pien (the reasons for acting cautiously) and hasten in our direction.")

The art of war teaches us to depend not on the chance that the enemy will not come, but on our own readiness to meet him; not on the hope that he won't attack, but on the certainty that we have made our position unassailable.

There are five dangerous flaws that may affect a general:

(1) Recklessness, which leads to destruction.

("Bravery without forethought," as Ts'ao Kung puts it, causes a man to fight blindly, like a mad bull. Chang Yu says, "Such an opponent should not be met with brute force but can be lured into an ambush and killed." Wu Tzŭ also points out that too much emphasis is often placed on a general's courage, forgetting that courage is just one of the qualities a general should have. A brave man who fights recklessly, without understanding what is truly advantageous, must be condemned. Ssu-ma Fa adds that "simply rushing to one's death does not guarantee victory.")

(2) Cowardice, which leads to capture.

(Ts'ao Kung explains that the word "cowardice" refers to someone "who is too timid to advance and seize an advantage." Wang Hsi adds that it describes someone who flees at the first sight of danger. Meng Shih gives a more detailed interpretation: "He is focused on surviving at all costs," meaning someone who avoids taking risks. But, as Sun Tzŭ knew, success in war often requires risk. T'ai Kung noted: "He who lets an advantage slip will eventually face real disaster." In 404 A.D., Liu Yu chased the rebel Huan Hsuan up the Yangtsze River. Though Liu Yu's forces were much smaller, Huan Hsuan, fearing the consequences of defeat, prepared a small boat attached to his warship for a quick escape. This lack of resolve destroyed his soldiers' morale. When the loyalists launched a determined attack using fireships, Huan Hsuan's forces were completely routed. They had to burn all their supplies and fled for two days without stopping. Chang Yu also tells a similar story of Chao Ying-ch'i, a general of the Chin State, who kept a boat ready during a battle with the Ch'u army in 597 B.C., so he could escape first if defeated.)

(3) A quick temper, which can be provoked by insults.

(Tu Mu tells the story of Yao Hsing, who in 357 A.D. was opposed by Huang Mei, Teng Ch'iang, and others. Yao Hsing shut himself inside his walls, refusing to engage. Teng Ch'iang, knowing Yao's fiery temper, suggested launching constant attacks to provoke him. He believed that Yao, once angered, would come out to fight. This strategy worked—Yao Hsiang left his defenses, was drawn into a trap as far as San-yuan by the enemy's fake retreat, and was ultimately defeated and killed.)

A delicate sense of honor that is easily wounded by shame is another potential fault.

This doesn't mean that a sense of honor is a flaw in a general. What Sun Tzŭ criticizes is being overly sensitive to slander or criticism, the kind of person who is too easily hurt by insults, even when they are undeserved. Mei Yao-ch'en wisely notes, though it may sound contradictory: "Those who seek glory should not worry too much about public opinion."

The fifth fault is being too concerned for the well-being of his men, which causes unnecessary worry and trouble.

Again, Sun Tzŭ isn't suggesting that a general should neglect the welfare of his soldiers. He simply means that focusing too much on their comfort can lead to poor decisions and lost opportunities. This short-term thinking can ultimately cause greater suffering for the troops in the long run because defeat, or a longer war, will be the result. A misguided sense of pity can lead a general to make choices that go against his better judgment, such as relieving a city under siege or sending reinforcements to a detachment under heavy pressure.

In the South African War, it's now accepted that our repeated attempts to relieve Ladysmith were strategic errors that failed to achieve their goal. In the end, it was the general who decided to stop letting sentiment for a small part of the army override the needs of the whole who finally succeeded. I recall an old soldier trying to defend one of our generals, who had notably failed during this war, by saying that he was "so kind to his men." In saying this, though he didn't realize it, he was actually condemning the general according to Sun Tzŭ's principles.

These are the five dangerous flaws in a general, which can ruin the conduct of war.

When an army is defeated and its leader is killed, the cause can almost always be traced back to one of these five flaws. Keep them in mind.

Chapter 9 - The Army on The March

Sun Tzu said: Now we turn to the important task of setting up camp and keeping a close eye on the enemy. When traveling through mountainous areas, it's important to move quickly across the mountains and stay near the valleys.

(This is because the dry, barren highlands can leave your troops without enough food or water. It's better to stay near places where water and grass are plentiful. Wu Tzu, an ancient military strategist, once said, "Don't camp in natural ovens," which means avoiding the entrances of valleys where the heat can become unbearable and where you could easily be trapped. Chang Yu provides a historical example: During the Later Han dynasty, a bandit named Wu-tu Ch'iang hid his troops in the hills. Instead of attacking directly, General Ma Yuan, who was sent to capture him, took control of the areas with water and other supplies. Ch'iang's troops soon ran out of provisions because they hadn't secured the valleys. With no access to resources, they were eventually forced to surrender.)

When choosing a campsite, always pick slightly higher ground.

(This doesn't mean the highest mountain peaks, but rather low hills that give you an advantage over the surrounding area. High ground lets you see the battlefield more easily and makes your camp less vulnerable to surprise attacks.)

It is also important to set up your camp so that it faces the sun.

(Some commentators, like Tu Mu, believed this meant facing south, while others, like Ch'en Hao, thought it meant facing east. Either way, the idea is that facing the sun gives your camp better visibility and warmth, making it more comfortable and easier to defend.)

In mountain warfare, one of the key rules is to never climb uphill to attack the enemy. It's better to hold the high ground and force the enemy to come to you. After crossing a river, always move away from it quickly.

(Ts'ao Kung explained this as a strategy to lure the enemy into crossing the river after you, where they will be more vulnerable. Chang Yu added that moving away from the river ensures that you have the freedom to maneuver, preventing the enemy from blocking your retreat or cutting off your supply lines.)

If the enemy is crossing a river, don't attack them while they're in the middle of the crossing. Wait until half of their forces have crossed, then strike.

(Li Ch'uan refers to Han Hsin's famous victory over Lung Chu at the Wei River as an example of this tactic.

Han Hsin's forces built a dam upstream at night and crossed the river to fake a retreat. Lung Chu, thinking Han Hsin's army was retreating in defeat, followed him across the river. At that moment, Han Hsin's troops broke the dam, sending a flood downstream that cut off Lung Chu's army. In the resulting chaos, Han Hsin's forces attacked decisively, killing Lung Chu and routing his army.)

If you're preparing to fight near a river the enemy hasn't crossed yet, don't position your troops too close to the river.

(Doing so could give the enemy the chance to plan a better crossing or force you into a defensive position when you could have set up an ambush instead.)

If you're stationed near a river, make sure to place your boats upstream from the enemy, and always keep your camp facing the sun.

(As mentioned before, being upstream gives you a tactical advantage, allowing you to control the flow of water. This applies whether your forces are on the riverbank or in boats. Facing the sun provides better visibility and can also give you a psychological advantage.)

Never move upstream to meet the enemy.

(Tu Mu warns that, since water flows downward, camping in a lower position is dangerous because the enemy could flood the river or poison the water and send it downstream to your camp. Chu-ko Wu-hou also advised against moving against the current in river warfare, as this would allow the enemy to use the natural flow of the river to their advantage.)

When it comes to river warfare, that's all you need to keep in mind. However, when crossing salt marshes, your only goal should be to get through them as quickly as possible.

(Salt marshes are inhospitable. They have little fresh water, the grass is scarce and not nutritious for animals, and the flat, open terrain leaves your forces vulnerable to attack.)

If you must fight in a salt marsh, camp near a source of fresh water and grass, and position your back against a group of trees.

(Li Ch'uan mentions that trees can signal safer ground, while Tu Mu points out that trees can protect your rear and reduce the chances of a surprise attack from the enemy.)

This concludes the rules for fighting in salt marshes. When fighting on flat, dry land, choose a position that is easy to access, with slightly rising ground on your right and behind you.

(Tu Mu quotes T'ai Kung, who recommended positioning your army with a stream or marsh on the left and a hill on the right. This setup offers natural defenses and strategic advantages.)

By following this rule, you will have danger in front of you and safety behind. This concludes the guidelines for warfare on flat land.

These principles of terrain management are the four essential branches of military strategy: (1) mountains, (2) rivers, (3) marshes, and (4) plains. Understanding these principles helped the Yellow Emperor defeat four kings.

(Some scholars question whether the Yellow Emperor truly defeated four kings, as historical records like the Shih Chi only mention his victories over Yen Ti and Ch'ih Yu. However, the Liu T'ao suggests he fought and won seventy battles, ultimately uniting the empire. Ts'ao Kung speculates that the Yellow Emperor established a feudal system with four princes holding the title of emperor. Meanwhile, Li Ch'uan believes that the art of war began with the Yellow Emperor, who learned it from his wise minister, Feng Hou.)

All armies prefer to occupy high ground rather than low ground because high ground offers advantages for both health and combat. Low ground, on the other hand, is often damp and unhealthy for troops.

(Ts'ao Kung advises generals to prioritize finding fresh water and good pasture for their animals to maintain the health and well-being of their forces.)

When choosing a campsite, look for hard, dry ground. This will help keep your soldiers healthy and reduce the risk of illness.

(Chang Yu adds that dry conditions help prevent diseases from spreading, which can be as dangerous as any enemy.)

Whenever possible, position yourself on the sunny side of a hill or slope, with the incline behind you and to your right. This will benefit your soldiers and allow you to make the best use of the natural terrain.

After heavy rains in higher regions, if you encounter a swollen river covered with foam, you must wait for the water to recede before attempting to cross.

Avoid areas with steep cliffs, narrow passes, or deep gorges with fast-flowing streams. These are natural traps—easy to enter but difficult to escape from. Places surrounded by steep banks or filled with water at the bottom should be avoided at all costs, as they are like natural prisons where you could easily be trapped.

(Dense forests with thick undergrowth, where spears cannot be used, should also be avoided, as well as quagmires and other soft ground that makes it difficult for chariots or horsemen to pass.)

While you should avoid such places, try to lead the enemy into them. If you face the enemy in such terrain, position them so that the natural obstacles are behind them, limiting their ability to maneuver.

If your camp is near hilly terrain, ponds surrounded by tall grasses, or woods with dense undergrowth, these areas must be thoroughly searched, as they are ideal hiding spots for enemy spies or ambushes.

When the enemy is nearby but remains still, it is a sign they are relying on the natural strength of their position. When they are distant and try to provoke a battle, they are likely trying to lure you out of your defensive position and into a trap.

If the enemy's camp seems easy to approach, be cautious—it may be a trap. Movement among trees in a forest is a sign that the enemy is advancing, likely cutting down trees to clear a path for their troops.

Birds suddenly taking flight may indicate an ambush. Startled animals could signal an impending attack.

If dust rises in a high column, it means chariots are approaching. If the dust is lower and spread out, infantry is on the move. Dust that moves in several directions suggests soldiers are gathering firewood, while small amounts of dust moving back and forth indicate the army is setting up camp.

When the enemy uses humble words but increases their preparations, it's a sign they are planning an attack. They may be pretending to be weak to make you feel secure.

If the enemy's camp looks humble but their preparations are intensifying, they are likely preparing for an assault. In one case, an army tried to demoralize its enemy by mutilating prisoners and desecrating graves, but this only strengthened the defenders' resolve. The defenders launched a clever counterattack by sending oxen with burning torches tied to their tails into the enemy's camp, causing chaos and helping them reclaim lost cities.

Aggressive words and forward movements often mean the enemy is preparing to retreat.

When light chariots are positioned on the flanks, it signals the enemy is getting ready for battle.

Peace offers that come without a sworn agreement usually signal a trap.

If the enemy's soldiers are running about and quickly forming up, the decisive moment is near.

If some soldiers advance while others retreat, it is likely a trick designed to confuse and mislead you.

Soldiers leaning on their spears are likely weak from hunger, and if they drink water immediately after getting it, the army is suffering from thirst.

If the enemy hesitates to act even when given an opportunity, it is a sign their troops are exhausted.

If birds are gathering in a specific area, it means that spot is unoccupied.

Noise at night suggests the enemy is anxious, while disorder in their camp indicates the general has lost control.

If the enemy's banners are being moved around frequently, it could mean there is rebellion in the ranks. Anger among the officers suggests that the soldiers are worn out.

When an army begins feeding its horses with grain, slaughtering cattle for food, and not hanging up its cooking pots, it means they are prepared to fight to the death.

When soldiers whisper in small groups, it indicates unrest in the ranks. Frequent rewards suggest the enemy is running low on resources, while excessive punishments point to severe internal problems.

If a general talks boldly but then hesitates out of fear of the enemy's numbers, it reveals a lack of intelligence. When envoys come with polite words, it usually means the enemy is seeking a truce.

If the enemy's troops stand facing yours for a long time without fighting or retreating, they may be preparing a surprise attack. Stay alert.

If your forces are roughly equal to the enemy's, you should be able to hold your position, but attacking head-on would be risky. Instead, gather your strength, watch the enemy closely, and wait for reinforcements.

A leader who underestimates the enemy and doesn't plan ahead will ultimately be defeated.

Punishing soldiers before they are loyal to you will lead to disobedience. However, if they are not disciplined after they become loyal, they will be ineffective in battle.

That's why it's important to first treat soldiers with kindness, then later enforce strict discipline. This is the path to victory.

If commands are enforced consistently, the army will be disciplined. If not, the soldiers will become disorderly. A general who trusts his men while making sure his orders are followed will strengthen both his

Chapter 10 - Terrain

Sun Tzŭ said: We can identify six kinds of terrain:

(1) Accessible ground;

(Mei Yao-ch'en explains this as ground that is well-supplied with roads and ways of communication.)

(2) Entangling ground;

(Mei Yao-ch'en describes this as "net-like" terrain, where if you enter, you may become entangled.)

(3) Temporizing ground;

(This is ground where you can delay or hold off.)

(4) Narrow passes; (5) Steep heights; (6) Positions far from the enemy.

(It is hardly necessary to point out the issues with this classification. There is a strange lack of logical reasoning in the unquestioning acceptance of these overlapping categories.)

Ground that both sides can freely move across is called accessible.

On this type of terrain, you should arrive before the enemy, take the higher, sunnier spots, and carefully guard your supply lines.

(The general meaning of this last phrase, as Tu Yu explains, is "not to allow the enemy to cut your communications." In view of Napoleon's statement, "the secret of war lies in the communications," it would have been helpful if Sun Tzŭ had elaborated more on this important subject here and in other sections. Col. Henderson says: "The line of supply is as vital to the life of an army as the heart is to a human being. Just as a duelist who finds his opponent's weapon threatening his life and his own guard out of place must adjust to his opponent's movements, the commander whose communications are suddenly threatened finds himself in a bad position. He may be forced to change all his plans, divide his forces into isolated groups, and fight with fewer troops on unprepared ground. In such a situation, defeat could mean the ruin or surrender of his entire army.")

If you follow these steps, you will be able to fight with an advantage.

Ground which can be abandoned but is hard to re-occupy is called entangling ground.

From a position of this sort, if the enemy is unprepared, you may sally forth and defeat him. But if the enemy is prepared for your coming, and you fail to defeat him, then, return being impossible, disaster will ensue.

When the position is such that neither side will gain by making the first move, it is called temporizing ground.

(Tu Mu says: "Each side finds it inconvenient to move, and the situation remains at a deadlock.")

In a position of this sort, even though the enemy should offer us an attractive bait,

(Tu Yu says, "turning their backs on us and pretending to flee." But this is only one of the lures which might induce us to quit our position.) it will be advisable not to stir forth, but rather to retreat, thus enticing the enemy in his turn; then, when part of his army has come out, we may deliver our attack with advantage.With regard to narrow passes, if you can occupy them first, let them be strongly garrisoned and await the advent of the enemy.

(Because then, as Tu Yu observes, "the initiative will lie with us, and by making sudden and unexpected attacks we shall have the enemy at our mercy.")

Should the enemy forestall you in occupying a pass, do not go after him if the pass is fully garrisoned, but only if it is weakly garrisoned.

With regard to precipitous heights, if you are beforehand with your adversary, you should occupy the raised and sunny spots, and there wait for him to come up.

(Ts'ao Kung says: "The particular advantage of securing heights and defiles is that your actions cannot then be dictated by the enemy." [For the enunciation of the grand principle alluded to, see VI. § 2]. Chang Yu tells the following anecdote of P'ei Hsing-chien

(A.D. 619-682), who was sent on a punitive expedition against the Turkic tribes. "At night he pitched his camp as usual, and it had already been completely fortified by wall and ditch, when suddenly he gave orders that the army should shift its quarters to a hill nearby. This was highly displeasing to his officers, who protested loudly against the extra fatigue which it would entail on the men. P'ei Hsing-chien, however, paid no heed to their remonstrances and had the camp moved as quickly as possible. The same night, a terrific storm came on, which flooded their former place of encampment to the depth of over twelve feet. The recalcitrant officers were amazed at the sight and owned that they had been in the wrong. 'How did you know what was going to happen?' they asked. P'ei Hsing-chien replied: 'From this time forward be content to obey orders without asking unnecessary questions.' From this it may be seen," Chang Yu continues, "that high and sunny places are advantageous not only for fighting, but also because they are immune from disastrous floods.")

If the enemy has occupied the high ground before you, do not pursue him, but instead retreat and try to lure him away.

(Li Shih-min's turning point in his campaign in 621 A.D. against the rebels Tou Chien-te, King of Hsia, and Wang Shih-ch'ung, Prince of Cheng, was his capture of the heights of Wu-lao. Despite this, Tou Chien-te still tried to help his ally in Lo-yang and was defeated and captured. See Chiu T'ang Shu, ch. 2, fol. 5 verso, and also ch. 54.)

If you are far from the enemy and the strength of both armies is equal, it is not easy to provoke a battle,

(The key is that you shouldn't undertake a long, tiring march, which would leave you exhausted while the enemy remains fresh and alert, as Tu Yu explains.) and fighting in such conditions will put you at a disadvantage.These six are the principles related to the terrain.

(Or, "principles relating to the ground." See I. § 8.)

A general in a position of responsibility must carefully study them.

Now, an army can face six different calamities, not due to natural causes, but because of the general's mistakes. These are: (1) Flight; (2) Insubordination; (3) Collapse; (4) Ruin; (5) Disorganization; (6) Rout.

If one force is thrown against another ten times its size, the outcome will be the flight of the smaller force.

When the common soldiers are too strong, and their officers are too weak, the result is insubordination.

(Tu Mu refers to the case of T'ien Pu [Hsin T'ang Shu, ch. 148], who was sent to Wei in 821 A.D. to lead an army against Wang T'ing-ts'ou. While he was in command, his soldiers treated him with disdain, openly disrespecting him by riding donkeys around the camp in large numbers. T'ien Pu couldn't control this behavior, and when he finally tried to engage the enemy, his troops scattered in all directions. Afterward, he tragically committed suicide.)

When the officers are too strong and the common soldiers too weak, the result is collapse.

(Ts'ao Kung says: "The officers are eager to advance, but the soldiers are weak and suddenly collapse.")

When higher-ranking officers act out of anger and fight the enemy on their own initiative, without waiting for the commander-in-chief to assess whether they are ready for battle, the result is ruin.

(Wang Hsi comments: "This refers to a general who becomes angry without reason and fails to recognize the capabilities of his subordinate officers. This leads to intense resentment and ultimately brings disaster upon him.")

When the general is weak and lacks authority, and when his orders are not clear or precise,

(Wei Liao Tzŭ in chapter 4 says: "If the commander gives his orders decisively, the soldiers will not need to hear them twice. If his actions are carried out without hesitation, the soldiers will not have doubts about following them." General Baden-Powell also emphasizes, saying: "The key to getting good results from your trained men lies in clear instructions." Wu Tzŭ, in chapter 3, adds: "The worst flaw in a military leader is indecision; the greatest disasters in an army come from hesitation.") when officers and men are not given specific duties,(Tu Mu explains: "Neither the officers nor the soldiers have any set routines.") and when the troops are assembled in a careless and disorganized manner, the result is complete chaos.When a general fails to properly assess the enemy's strength and sends a smaller force against a much larger one, or orders a weak unit to engage a stronger force without placing the best soldiers at the front, the outcome will be a disastrous defeat.

(Chang Yu explains this by saying: "Whenever there is fighting, the most determined soldiers should be placed at the front, both to inspire confidence in our own troops and to intimidate the enemy." This concept aligns with Caesar's use of the primi ordines in "De Bello Gallico," V. 28, 44, and elsewhere.)

These are six ways to invite defeat, and they must be carefully observed by any general who holds a position of responsibility.

(See earlier discussion in § 13.)

The natural landscape is the soldier's greatest ally;

(Ch'en Hao notes: "The advantages of weather and timing are not as significant as those related to the terrain.") but the ability to assess the enemy, control the factors that lead to victory, and accurately judge difficulties, dangers, and distances is what defines a truly great general.He who knows these principles and in fighting puts his knowledge into practice, will win his battles. He who knows them not, nor practises them, will surely be defeated.

If fighting is sure to result in victory, then you must fight, even though the ruler forbids it; if fighting will not result in victory, then you must not fight even at the ruler's bidding.

(Chang Yu also quotes the saying: "Decrees from the Son of Heaven do not penetrate the walls of a camp." Huang Shih-kung of the Ch'in dynasty, who is said to have been the patron of Chang Liang and to have written the San Lueh, has these words attributed to him: "The responsibility of setting an army in motion must devolve on the general alone; if advance and retreat are controlled from the Palace, brilliant results will hardly be achieved. Hence the god-like ruler and the enlightened monarch are content to play a humble part in furthering their country's cause [literally, kneel down to push the chariot wheel]." This means that "in matters lying outside the zenana, the decision of the military commander must be absolute.")

The general who advances without coveting fame and retreats without fearing disgrace,

(It was Wellington, I think, who said that the hardest thing of all for a soldier is to retreat.) whose only thought is to protect his country and do good service for his sovereign, is the jewel of the kingdom.(A noble presentiment, in few words, of the Chinese “happy warrior.” Such a man, says Ho Shih, “even if he had to suffer punishment, would not regret his conduct.”)

Regard your soldiers as your children, and they will follow you into the deepest valleys; look on them as your own beloved sons, and they will stand by you even unto death.

(Cf. I. § 6. In this connection, Tu Mu draws for us an engaging picture of the famous general Wu Ch'i, from whose treatise on war I have frequently had occasion to quote: “He wore the same clothes and ate the same food as the meanest of his soldiers, refused to have either a horse to ride or a mat to sleep on, carried his own surplus rations wrapped in a parcel, and shared every hardship with his men. One of his soldiers was suffering from an abscess, and Wu Ch'i himself sucked out the virus. The soldier's mother, hearing this, began wailing and lamenting. Somebody asked her, saying: 'Why do you cry? Your son is only a common soldier, and yet the commander-in-chief himself has sucked the poison from his sore.' The woman replied, 'Many years ago, Lord Wu performed a similar service for my husband, who never left him afterwards, and finally met his death at the hands of the enemy. And now that he has done the same for my son, he too will fall fighting I know not where."')

Li Ch'uan mentions the Viscount of Ch'u, who invaded the small state of Hsiao during the winter. The Duke of Shen said to him: "Many of the soldiers are suffering severely from the cold." So he made a round of the whole army, comforting and encouraging the men; and straightway they felt as if they were clothed in garments lined with floss silk.

If, however, you are lenient but unable to assert your authority; kind-hearted but unable to enforce your commands; and also incapable of maintaining order, then your soldiers will be like spoiled children—they will be useless in any real situation.

[Li Ching once said that if you could make your soldiers fear you, they wouldn't be afraid of the enemy. Tu Mu recounts a strict example of military discipline from 219 A.D., when Lu Meng was holding the town of Chiang-ling. He had ordered his army not to bother the local people or take anything from them by force. However, one officer under his command, who happened to be from the same town, took a bamboo hat from a villager to wear over his helmet in the rain. Despite being a fellow townsman, Lu Meng didn't excuse the breach of discipline. He ordered the officer's execution, though tears fell down his face as he gave the command. This strict action instilled a healthy sense of fear in the army, and from that point on, even items left in the road were not touched.]

If we know our own men are ready to attack but don't know that the enemy is not vulnerable to attack, we've only come halfway to victory.

[As Ts'ao Kung says, "in this case, the outcome is uncertain."]

If we know the enemy is vulnerable but don't realize that our own men aren't ready to attack, we've again only come halfway to victory.

If we know the enemy is vulnerable, and we know our men are ready to attack, but we don't realize that the terrain makes fighting impossible, we're still only halfway to victory.

Hence, the seasoned soldier, once on the move, is never confused; once he breaks camp, he is never lost.

[According to Tu Mu, this is because he has planned everything so thoroughly that victory is ensured before any action is taken. Chang Yu adds, "He doesn't act rashly, so when he does move, he makes no mistakes."]

Thus the saying goes: If you know the enemy and know yourself, you won't have to worry about the outcome of a hundred battles; if you know both Heaven and Earth, your victory will be complete.

[Li Ch'uan concludes: "If you understand three

things—the affairs of men, the seasons of Heaven, and the natural advantages of Earth—, you will always win your battles."]

Chapter 11 - The Nine Situations

Sun Tzu said: The art of war recognizes nine types of ground: (1) Dispersive ground; (2) facile ground; (3) contentious ground; (4) open ground; (5) ground of intersecting highways; (6) serious ground; (7) difficult ground; (8) hemmed-in ground; (9) desperate ground.

When a leader is fighting in his own territory, it is called dispersive ground. This is because the soldiers, being near their homes and eager to see their wives and children, are likely to seize the opportunity of a battle to scatter in every direction. As Tu Mu explains, "They will lack the desperation needed to fight with full valor, and when they retreat, they will find places of refuge."

When the army has crossed into enemy territory, but not deeply, it is called facile ground. Li Ch'uan and Ho Shih say this is because retreat is still easy, and other commentators give similar explanations. Tu Mu adds, "When your army has crossed the border, you should burn your boats and bridges to show everyone there is no turning back."

Ground that offers great advantage to either side is called contentious ground. Tu Mu defines this as ground "worth fighting for." Ts'ao Kung says it is ground "on which the few and weak can defeat the many and strong," such as "the neck of a pass," which Li Ch'uan mentions as an example. Thermopylae fits this description because holding it for even a short time delayed an entire invading army, providing invaluable time. As Wu Tzu says in his writings: "When facing odds of one against ten, there is nothing better than a narrow pass."

When Lu Kuang was returning from his successful expedition to Turkestan in 385 A.D., and had reached I-ho with many spoils, Liang Hsi, the administrator of Liang-chou, took advantage of the death of Fu Chien, King of Ch'in, to plot against him. Yang Han, governor of Kao-ch'ang, advised him, saying, "Lu Kuang has just won victories in the west, and his soldiers are strong and confident. If we face him in the desert sands, we will not stand a chance. Instead, let's take control of the defile at the mouth of the Kao-wu pass. By cutting off his water supply, we can wait until his troops are weakened by thirst and then dictate our terms. Or, if that pass is too far, we could confront him at the I-wu pass, which is closer. Even a skilled strategist like Tzŭ-fang could not overcome the strength of these two positions." Liang Hsi, however, refused this advice and was overwhelmed and defeated by the invader.

Ground where both sides can move freely is called open ground.

[There are different interpretations of the word used for this type of ground. Ts'ao Kung says it means "ground covered with roads, like a chessboard." Ho Shih suggests it means "ground where communication is easy."]

Ground that forms the key to three neighboring states is ground of intersecting highways.

[Ts'au Kung defines this as "our country next to the enemy's, with a third country adjoining both." Meng Shih uses the example of Cheng, a small state bordered by Ch'i to the northeast, Chin to the west, and Ch'u to the south.]

Whoever takes control of this area first has a strategic advantage over most of the region.

[The one who holds this important position can force many neighboring states to become allies.]

When an army has moved deep into enemy territory, leaving fortified cities behind, it is on serious ground.

[Wang Hsi says it is called serious ground because "the army's situation becomes serious when it reaches this point."]

Mountain forests, steep terrain, marshes, and fens—all areas that are difficult to pass—are called difficult ground.

Ground that is reached through narrow gorges, where retreat can only happen through winding paths, and where a small enemy force could easily defeat a large army, is called hemmed-in ground.

Ground where the only way to avoid destruction is to fight immediately is called desperate ground.

[The situation, as described by Ts'ao Kung, is much like hemmed-in ground but worse, with no way out: "A tall mountain in front, a large river behind, no way to advance, no way to retreat." Ch'en Hao says being on desperate ground is "like sitting in a sinking boat or standing in a burning house." Tu Mu shares a vivid description from Li Ching of an army caught in this type of trap: "Imagine an army in enemy territory with no local guides. The army stumbles into a deadly trap, at the enemy's mercy. A ravine on the left, a mountain on the right, and a path so dangerous that horses must be tied together and chariots lifted with slings. There's no way forward, and retreat is blocked. The soldiers move in single file, barely forming ranks before an overwhelming enemy force appears. There's no time to rest, no escape. We try to fight, but there's no space; we try to defend ourselves, but there's no respite. Staying put means wasting time, but any move invites enemy attacks from the front and rear. The land is wild, with no food or water. The soldiers are exhausted, the horses worn out, and every effort seems hopeless. The path is so narrow that one person could stop an army of ten thousand. The enemy controls all the advantages, while we have lost all our options. Even with the bravest soldiers and sharpest weapons, how could they possibly be effective?" Students of Greek history may recall the tragic end of the Sicilian expedition and the suffering of the Athenians under Nicias and Demosthenes. [See Thucydides, VII. 78 sqq.]]

Do not fight on ground where you're scattered. Do not stop on easy ground. Do not attack when there's a lot of opposition.

[Instead, focus all your energy on getting the upper hand first. So says Ts'ao Kung. However, Li Ch'uan and others believe this means the enemy has already beaten us to it, so attacking would be foolish. In the Sun Tzŭ Hsu Lu, when the King of Wu asks what to do in this situation, Sun Tzŭ responds: "The rule for contested ground is that whoever holds the ground first has the advantage. If the enemy has secured this type of position, do not attack. Trick them into moving by pretending to flee—show your flags and beat your drums—rush to other spots they can't afford to lose—drag branches and kick up dust—confuse their senses—send your best troops to secretly ambush them. Then your enemy will rush out to save the situation."]

On open ground, don't try to block the enemy's path.

[Because it would be pointless and would put the blocking force in danger. There are two interpretations here. I follow Chang Yu's view. The other is found in Ts'ao Kung's short note: "Come closer together"—which means making sure part of your army isn't cut off.]

On ground with crossing roads, join up with your allies.

[Or perhaps, "make alliances with neighboring states."]

On serious ground, take what you need.

[Li Ch'uan adds an interesting note: "When an army moves deep into enemy territory, it's important not to anger the local people by treating them unfairly. Follow the example of the Han Emperor Kao Tsu, who during his march into Ch'in territory didn't harm women or steal valuables. [Note: this was in 207 B.C., a lesson that could embarrass Christian armies that marched into Peking in 1900 A.D.] This is how he won the hearts of the people. In this passage, I think the right reading is not 'take what you need,' but 'don't take what you don't need.' Sadly, the commentator's emotions may have clouded his judgment. Tu Mu, at least, isn't under any such illusions. He says: 'When camped on serious ground, where there's no reason to advance and no chance to retreat, one should prepare for a long defense by gathering supplies from all around, while keeping a close watch on the enemy.'"]

In tough terrain, keep moving steadily forward.

[Or, in the words of VIII. § 2, "don't stop and make camp."]

When trapped, use a clever strategy.

[Ts'ao Kung says, "Try something unusual or unexpected," and Tu Yu adds, "In such situations, you must come up with a plan that fits the moment. If you can trick the enemy, you might escape the danger." This is exactly what happened when Hannibal was trapped in the mountains on the road to Casilinum, seemingly caught by the dictator Fabius. Hannibal came up with a clever trick, similar to one used by T'ien Tan 62 years earlier. [See IX. § 24, note.] At nightfall, they tied bundles of twigs to the horns of around 2,000 oxen and set them on fire. The terrified animals were driven towards the mountain passes held by the enemy. The sight of these fast-moving lights frightened the Romans, causing them to retreat, and Hannibal's army safely passed through the narrow pass. [See Polybius, III. 93, 94; Livy, XXII. 16, 17.]]

When in desperate situations, fight.

[As Chia Lin notes, "If you fight with everything you've got, you have a chance to survive. But if you just stay in your corner, death is certain."]

In the past, skilled leaders knew how to divide the enemy's front from their rear;

[In more exact terms, "They would make sure the front and rear were no longer in touch with each other."]

They knew how to stop the enemy's big and small divisions from working together, and how to prevent strong troops from saving the weak, and officers from rallying their soldiers.

When the enemy's troops were scattered, they made sure the enemy couldn't regroup. Even when the enemy's forces were united, they still managed to keep them disorganized.

When it was to their advantage, they moved forward; if not, they stayed put.

[Mei Yao-ch'en links this to the previous point: "After successfully disrupting the enemy, they would advance to secure any advantage; if there was no advantage, they would stay where they were."]

If asked how to handle a large, organized enemy force about to launch an attack, I would say: "Start by capturing something your opponent values; this will force him to act according to your will."

[There are different views on what Sun Tzŭ meant here. Ts'ao Kung thinks it refers to "some strategic advantage the enemy relies on." Tu Mu says: "The three things an enemy is eager to do, and on which his success depends, are: (1) to capture our key positions; (2) to destroy our farmlands; and (3) to protect his own supply lines." Our goal should be to disrupt his plans in these three areas, rendering him powerless. [Cf. III. § 3.] By boldly seizing the initiative, you force the enemy into a defensive position.]

Speed is the essence of war.

[Tu Mu explains, "This is a summary of the main principles of warfare," and adds, "These are the deepest truths of military science, and the general's most important duty." The following stories, told by Ho Shih, show how important speed was to two of China's greatest generals. In 227 A.D., Meng Ta, governor of Hsin-ch'eng under the Wei Emperor Wen Ti, was planning to defect to the House of Shu, and had begun communicating with Chu-ko Liang, the Prime Minister of that state. The Wei general Ssu-ma I, who was then the military governor of Wan, heard about Meng Ta's treachery and immediately set out with an army to stop him, after having tricked him with a friendly message. Ssu-ma's officers suggested that they should investigate more thoroughly before making a move. Ssu-ma I replied, "Meng Ta is an unreliable man, and we should go and punish him right away, while he is still uncertain and before he has fully betrayed us." Then, with a series of forced marches, he brought his army to the walls of Hsin-ch'eng in just eight days. Now, Meng Ta had earlier written in a letter to Chu-ko Liang: "Wan is 1,200 li from here. When news of my revolt reaches Ssu-ma I, he will inform the emperor, but it will take a whole month before any action is taken. By that time, my city will be well fortified. Besides, Ssu-ma I is not likely to come himself, and the generals that will be sent are not worth worrying about." But his next letter was full of panic: "Though only eight days have passed since I revolted, an army is already at the gates. What incredible speed!" Two weeks later, Hsin-ch'eng fell, and Meng Ta was executed. [See Chin Shu, ch. 1, f. 3.] In 621 A.D., Li Ching was sent from K'uei-chou in Ssu-ch'uan to defeat the rebel Hsiao Hsien, who had declared himself Emperor in the modern-day Ching-chou Fu in Hupeh. It was autumn, and the Yangtze River was in flood, so Hsiao Hsien did not expect Li Ching to risk coming down through the gorges, and as a result made no preparations. But Li Ching immediately prepared his army and was about to set off when the other generals begged him to delay his departure until the river was less dangerous to navigate. Li Ching replied, "For a soldier, overwhelming speed is of the utmost importance, and he must never miss an opportunity. Now is the time to strike, before Hsiao Hsien even knows we have gathered an army. If we attack while the river is in flood, we will reach his capital with such unexpected speed, like thunder that is heard before you have time to cover your ears." [See VII. § 19, note.] This is a key principle of war. Even if Hsiao Hsien hears of our approach, he will have to raise his soldiers in such a rush that they will not be fit to fight us. This way, we will secure total victory." Everything happened as predicted, and Hsiao Hsien was forced to surrender, nobly asking that his people be spared and he alone face death.]

Take advantage of the enemy's lack of readiness, move by unexpected routes, and attack where they are not guarded.

Here are the principles for an invading force to follow: The deeper you go into a country, the stronger the unity among your troops will become, and the defenders will struggle to defeat you.

Make raids in fertile lands to provide your army with food.

[Cf. § 13. Li Ch'uan does not provide a note here.]

Pay close attention to the well-being of your soldiers,

[By "well-being," Wang Hsi means, "Take good care of them, indulge them, make sure they have enough food and drink, and generally keep them in good condition."] and do not overwork them. Focus your energy and save your strength.[Ch'en recalls the approach used in 224 B.C. by the brilliant general Wang Chien, whose leadership was key to the First Emperor's success. He invaded the Ch'u State, where a mass mobilization had been raised against him. However, uncertain about the mood of his troops, he refused to engage in battle and stayed strictly on the defensive. The Ch'u general tried repeatedly to provoke a fight, but day after day, Wang Chien remained inside his fortifications. Instead of rushing into battle, he focused on winning the trust and loyalty of his soldiers. He ensured they were well-fed, even sharing meals with them, provided opportunities for bathing, and used every possible method to keep them content and united. After some time, he sent people to check on how his soldiers were spending their free time. The report came back that they were competing in activities like weightlifting and long jumping. When Wang Chien heard this, he knew their morale was high, and they were ready for battle. By then, the Ch'u army, frustrated by their unanswered challenges, had marched away to the east. At that moment, Wang Chien broke camp and pursued them. In the battle that followed, the Ch'u forces were crushed, and shortly after, the entire state of Ch'u was conquered by Ch'in, with their king, Fu-ch'u, taken captive.]

Keep your army constantly on the move,

[So the enemy never knows where you are. However, it has occurred to me that the true meaning might be "link your army together."] and develop plans that are impossible for the enemy to understand.Put your soldiers in positions where there is no escape, and they will choose death over retreat. If they are ready to face death, there is nothing they cannot accomplish.

[Chang Yu quotes Wei Liao Tzŭ (ch. 3): "If a single man ran wild with a sword in a marketplace, and everyone else fled from him, it wouldn't mean that he alone was brave and the rest were cowards. The truth is, a man with nothing to lose and a man who values his life are not in the same position."]

Both officers and soldiers will give their full strength.

[Chang Yu says: "If they find themselves in a difficult situation together, they will definitely combine their strength to get out of it."]

When soldiers are in desperate situations, they lose all sense of fear. If they have nowhere to run, they will stand firm. If they are deep in enemy territory, they will fight with determination. If there is no other option, they will fight fiercely.

Thus, without needing to be organized, soldiers will always be alert; without needing to be asked, they will follow your orders.

[Literally, "Without asking, you will receive."]

Without strict rules, they will stay loyal; without needing commands, they can be trusted.

Ban the taking of omens, and eliminate superstitious doubts. Then, until the moment of death, no disaster will be feared.

[Superstition and fear can turn men into cowards who "die many times before their deaths." Tu Mu quotes Huang Shih-kung: "Spells and incantations should be strictly forbidden, and no officer should inquire about the fate of the army through divination, as this can unsettle the soldiers' minds." He continues, "If all doubts and superstitions are cast aside, your soldiers will remain resolute until the very end."]

If our soldiers are not burdened with wealth, it is not because they dislike riches; if their lives are not overly long, it is not because they do not want longevity.

[Chang Yu explains this well: "Wealth and long life are natural desires for all men. So, if soldiers burn or throw away valuables and give up their lives, it is not because they hate them, but because they have no choice." Sun Tzŭ hints that since soldiers are only human, it is the general's responsibility to make sure they are not tempted to avoid battle and seek riches instead.]

On the day your soldiers are ordered to battle, they may cry,

[The word used here is "snivel," which suggests deeper sorrow than just tears.] some of them sitting up and soaking their clothes with tears, while others lying down let the tears roll down their faces.[This isn't because they are afraid, but because, as Ts'ao Kung says, "they have all made a firm decision to fight to the death." We can also remember that the heroes of the Iliad were similarly open in showing their emotions. Chang Yu references the sad farewell at the I River between Ching K'o and his friends, when Ching K'o was sent to assassinate the King of Ch'in (who would later become the First Emperor) in 227 B.C. As he said goodbye, tears flowed like rain, and he recited these lines: "The wind blows sharp, the river is cold; Your hero goes forth—never to return."]

But when they are cornered, they will show the courage of a Chu or a Kuei.

[Chu was the personal name of Chuan Chu, a native of the Wu State and a contemporary of Sun Tzŭ. He was hired by Kung-tzu Kuang, also known as Ho Lu Wang, to assassinate the king Wang Liao with a dagger hidden inside a fish at a banquet. He succeeded, but was immediately cut down by the king's guards. This happened in 515 B.C. The other hero, Ts'ao Kuei (also known as Ts'ao Mo), became famous 166 years earlier, in 681 B.C. After Lu had been defeated three times by Ch'i, they were about to sign a treaty giving up a large part of their territory. At that moment, Ts'ao Kuei grabbed Huan Kung, the Duke of Ch'i, at the altar and held a dagger to his chest. None of the Duke's men dared move, and Ts'ao Kuei demanded that all of Lu's territory be returned, arguing that Lu was unfairly treated because it was smaller and weaker. Fearing for his life, Huan Kung agreed. Ts'ao Kuei then calmly put away his dagger and sat back down, showing no fear. Although the Duke wanted to break the agreement later, his wise counselor Kuan Chung advised him that it would be unwise to go back on his word. As a result, Lu regained all the land they had lost in the three battles.]

A skilled strategist can be compared to the shuai-jan. The shuai-jan is a snake found in the Ch'ang mountains.

["Shuai-jan" means "suddenly" or "rapidly," and the snake got this name because of how quickly it moves. Over time, the term came to refer to military maneuvers.]

If you strike at its head, its tail will attack you; if you strike at its tail, its head will attack you; if you strike at its middle, both head and tail will attack you together.

If asked whether an army can be made to act like the shuai-jan,

[As Mei Yao-ch'en says, "Is it possible to make the front and rear of an army respond quickly to an attack on the other, just as if they were parts of one living body?"]

I would answer, Yes. The men of Wu and the men of Yüeh are enemies;

[Cf. VI. § 21.] yet if they are crossing a river in the same boat and a storm strikes, they will help each other, just as the left hand helps the right.[The meaning is: If two enemies will cooperate when faced with a shared danger, how much more should two parts of the same army, bound together by shared interests and camaraderie, work together? Still, it is well known that many campaigns have been lost because of a lack of cooperation, especially when allied armies are involved.]

Therefore, it is not enough to rely on tethering horses or burying chariot wheels in the ground to keep an army from fleeing.

[These strange methods, meant to stop soldiers from running away, remind us of the Athenian hero Sophanes, who carried an anchor into battle at Plataea and used it to tie himself to one spot. [See Herodotus, IX. 74.] Sun Tzŭ is saying that merely making flight impossible through such mechanical means is not enough. You will only succeed if your men have strong willpower, unity of purpose, and, most importantly, a spirit of cooperation. This is the lesson we can learn from the shuai-jan.]

The way to manage an army is to set one standard of courage that everyone must meet.

[Literally, "make the courage of all equal as if it were that of one." If the ideal army is to act as one cohesive unit, then the determination and spirit of its members must be of the same quality, or at least not below a certain level. Wellington's comment about his army at Waterloo, calling it "the worst he had ever commanded," was likely a reflection of its lack of this essential trait—unity of courage and spirit. If he hadn't anticipated the Belgian defections and kept those troops in the background, he almost certainly would have lost the battle.]

How to make the best use of both strong and weak soldiers is a matter of how you use the terrain.

[Mei Yao-ch'en explains: "The way to erase the differences between strong and weak and make both useful is by using the natural features of the ground." Weaker troops, if placed in strong defensive positions, can hold out as effectively as better troops on more vulnerable ground. A good position can make up for a lack of stamina and courage. Col. Henderson comments: "With all due respect to textbooks and standard tactics, I believe the study of terrain is often neglected, and that too little attention is given to the selection of positions and the great benefits that come from using natural features, whether attacking or defending." [2]]

Thus, the skillful general leads his army as easily as if he were leading a single person by the hand, whether they want to follow or not.

[Tu Mu says: "The comparison refers to how easily this is done."]

A general must stay calm to ensure secrecy and be upright and just to maintain order.

He must be able to confuse his officers and soldiers with false reports and deceptive appearances,

[Literally, "to deceive their eyes and ears."] so that they remain in complete ignorance of his true plans. [Ts'ao Kung gives a wise saying: "Troops should not be allowed to know your plans at the beginning; they may only share in your success when it is achieved." One of the key principles of war is "to mystify, mislead, and surprise the enemy." But how about deceiving your own troops? Those who think Sun Tzŭ overstates this would benefit from reading Col. Henderson's comments on Stonewall Jackson's Valley campaign: "The great care Jackson took to hide his movements, intentions, and thoughts, even from his most trusted staff officers, would have been seen as unnecessary by a less meticulous commander." [3] In 88 A.D., according to ch. 47 of the Hou Han Shu, Pan

Ch'ao led 25,000 men from Khotan and other Central Asian states to attack Yarkand. The King of Kutcha sent his commander with 50,000 troops from Wen-su, Ku-mo, and Wei-t'ou to defend it. Pan Ch'ao called a war council with his officers and the King of Khotan and said, 'We are outnumbered and cannot defeat the enemy directly. The best plan is to split up and go in different directions. The King of Khotan will march east, and I will head west. We will leave after the evening drum sounds.' Pan Ch'ao secretly released some prisoners, who informed the King of Kutcha of these plans. Feeling confident, the King of Kutcha took 10,000 horsemen to block Pan Ch'ao's retreat in the west, while the King of Wen-su led 8,000 cavalry east to intercept the King of Khotan. Once Pan Ch'ao knew the enemy leaders had left, he quickly reunited his troops and launched a surprise attack at dawn on Yarkand's camp. The enemy fled in confusion, and Pan Ch'ao pursued them, killing over 5,000 and seizing many horses, cattle, and other valuables. After Yarkand surrendered, Kutcha and the other states withdrew their forces. From then on, Pan Ch'ao's influence dominated the western regions." In this case, the Chinese general not only kept his officers in the dark about his real plans, but also used the bold tactic of splitting his army to deceive the enemy.]

By altering his tactics and changing his plans,

[Wang Hsi believes this means not using the same strategy twice.] he keeps the enemy unsure and without clear information.[Chang Yu, in a quote from another work, says: "The idea that war is based on deception doesn't only apply to tricking the enemy. You must also deceive your own soldiers. Make them follow you without letting them know the reasons behind your decisions."]

By shifting his camp and taking indirect routes, he prevents the enemy from predicting his intentions.

At the crucial moment, the leader of an army acts like someone who has climbed a high wall and then kicks away the ladder behind him. He takes his soldiers deep into enemy territory before revealing his true plans.

[Literally, "releases the spring" (see V. § 15), meaning that he takes a decisive action that makes retreat impossible—similar to Hsiang Yu, who sank his ships after crossing a river. Ch'en Hao, followed by Chia Lin, interprets this less clearly as "uses every trick at his disposal."]

He burns his boats and destroys his cooking pots; like a shepherd driving a flock of sheep, he directs his soldiers this way and that, and no one knows where they are headed.

[Tu Mu says: "The army only understands orders to advance or retreat; it doesn't know the true goals of attacking or conquering."]

To gather his forces and lead them into danger—this is the duty of a general.

[Sun Tzŭ means that once the army is mobilized, there should be no delay in striking at the enemy's core. Note how he returns to this idea again and again. In the warring states of ancient China, desertion was likely a much more immediate and serious threat than in today's armies.]

The different strategies suitable for the nine types of ground;

[Chang Yu says: "One should not rigidly apply the rules for the nine types of ground."] the need for either aggressive or defensive tactics, and the basic laws of human nature: these are things that must absolutely be studied.When invading hostile territory, the general principle is that penetrating deeply creates unity, while penetrating only a little leads to division.

[Cf. § 20.]

When you leave your homeland and lead your army into neighboring lands, you are on critical ground.

This kind of ground is mentioned earlier, but it is not listed among the Nine Situations or the Six Calamities in another chapter. At first glance, you might think it means "distant ground," but according to commentators, this is not correct. Mei Yao-ch'en explains that it's ground that is neither far enough to be called "easy" nor close enough to be "scattered." It is somewhere in between. Wang Hsi says that it is ground separated from home by a state whose territory we had to cross to reach it, so it is important to finish our task there quickly. He adds that this situation is rare, which is why it is not included among the Nine Situations.

When you have roads in all directions, it is ground of intersecting highways.

When you go deep into enemy territory, it is serious ground. When you advance only a little, it is easy ground.

When the enemy's strongholds are behind you, and narrow paths are in front, it is hemmed-in ground. When there is no place to retreat, it is desperate ground.

Therefore, on scattered ground, I would unite my men under a common goal.

To achieve this, Tu Mu suggests staying on the defensive and avoiding battle.

On easy ground, I would keep all parts of my army closely connected.

Tu Mu explains that this is to prevent two dangers: the possibility of soldiers deserting or a sudden enemy attack. Mei Yao-ch'en adds that during the march, the troops should stay close together, and in camp, the fortifications should be continuous.

On contested ground, I would hurry to bring up my rear forces.

Ts'ao Kung offers this view, and Chang Yu agrees, saying that the head and tail of the army must reach their destination together without straggling. Mei Yao-ch'en suggests another view: If the enemy hasn't yet reached the desired position and we are behind them, we should move quickly to claim it. Ch'en Hao takes another approach, thinking the enemy may have already chosen their ground. He quotes a passage where Sun Tzŭ warns against attacking when exhausted. If a favorable position lies ahead, Ch'en Hao advises sending a strong unit to secure it, and if the enemy tries to fight for it, the main force can strike their rear, leading to victory.

On open ground, I would stay alert and defend carefully. On ground of intersecting highways, I would strengthen my alliances.

On serious ground, I would make sure to maintain a steady flow of supplies.

Commentators believe this refers to gathering forage and plunder, not maintaining a connection with home, as you might expect.

On difficult ground, I would keep moving forward.

On hemmed-in ground, I would block any escape routes.

Meng Shih explains that this would make it seem like I am defending the position, but my real plan is to break through the enemy's lines unexpectedly. Mei Yao-ch'en adds that this would make my soldiers fight with desperation. Wang Hsi suggests that this would prevent my men from being tempted to flee. Tu Mu points out that this is the opposite of a previous situation, where it is the enemy who is surrounded. An example of this is from 532 A.D., when Kao Huan, who later became Emperor, was surrounded by a much larger army led by Erh-chu Chao and others. Despite his smaller force, which included only 2000 horsemen and fewer than 30,000 foot soldiers, Kao Huan blocked all remaining escape routes by driving oxen and donkeys into the gaps. When his officers and men saw there was no escape, they fought with extraordinary bravery and broke through the enemy ranks with fierce determination.

On desperate ground, I would tell my soldiers there is no hope of survival.

Tu Yu suggests making it clear to the soldiers that survival is impossible by burning their baggage, throwing away supplies, blocking wells, and destroying cooking stoves. The only way to live is to fight as if they expect to die. Mei Yao-ch'en adds that their only chance of survival is to abandon all hope of it.

This concludes what Sun Tzŭ says about "grounds"

and their corresponding "variations." Reviewing these passages, it is clear that the subject is treated in a somewhat scattered and unstructured manner. Sun Tzŭ begins by listing a few variations before discussing "grounds" but only mentions five variations, which are later expanded. Some types of ground are addressed earlier, while chapter X introduces six new types of ground, each with a variation to match. However, none of these six types are revisited, and one closely resembles a type of ground described later. In chapter XI, we encounter the Nine Grounds, followed by a list of their variations. By sections 43-45, new definitions for several of these grounds are provided, as well as for another type not previously mentioned. Finally, the nine variations are listed again, though many of them differ from earlier versions.

Although we cannot definitively explain the current state of Sun Tzŭ's text, a few interesting observations stand out: (1) Chapter VIII is titled "Nine Variations," but only five are listed. (2) This chapter is unusually short. (3) Chapter XI is called "The Nine Grounds," but some of the grounds are defined more than once, and two separate lists of variations are given. (4) This chapter is much longer than any other, except chapter IX. While no specific conclusions can be drawn from these facts, it seems likely that Sun Tzŭ's work has not reached us exactly as he originally wrote it. Chapter

VIII appears incomplete and possibly out of place, while chapter XI contains material that may have been added later or misplaced from another part of the text.

For it is the soldier's nature to offer a determined resistance when surrounded, to fight fiercely when there is no way out, and to follow orders quickly when faced with danger. Chang Yu refers to the actions of Pan Ch'ao's loyal followers in 73 A.D. The story is found in the Hou Han Shu, chapter 47: "When Pan Ch'ao arrived at Shan-shan, the king, Kuang, initially treated him with great politeness and respect; but soon after, his attitude changed abruptly, and he became negligent and indifferent. Pan Ch'ao spoke of this to the officers with him: 'Have you noticed,' he said, 'that Kuang's courtesy is fading? This must mean that envoys from the Northern barbarians have arrived, leaving him uncertain about which side to support. That is surely the reason. The wise man, we are told, can foresee events before they happen; how much more easily can he observe what is already taking place!' Then he called one of the locals assigned to his service and set a trap by asking, 'Where are those envoys from the Hsiung-nu who arrived a few days ago?' The man, startled and afraid, quickly revealed the whole truth. Pan Ch'ao, having secured the man, then summoned a meeting with his officers, thirty-six in all, and began drinking with them. As the wine took effect, he encouraged their spirits further by saying: 'Gentlemen, here we are in a remote region, eager to achieve riches and honor through a great deed. Recently, an ambassador from the Hsiung-nu has arrived, and because of this, the respectful treatment we've received from the king has faded. If this envoy persuades him to capture us and deliver us to the Hsiung-nu, our bones will be left for the wolves of the desert. What are we to do?' The officers, as one, replied, 'With our lives at risk, we will follow you through life and death.' The rest of this story can be found in chapter twelve, section one."

We cannot form alliances with neighboring rulers until we understand their intentions. We are not fit to lead an army on the march unless we know the landscape—its mountains and forests, its traps and cliffs, its marshes and swamps. We cannot make use of the land's advantages unless we employ local guides. These three statements are repeated from chapter seven to stress their importance, according to the commentators. However, I believe they are placed here as a lead-in to the next statements. Regarding local guides, Sun Tzŭ might have added that there is always a risk of error, either due to their betrayal or through misunderstanding. Livy, for instance, recounts a case where Hannibal ordered a guide to take him near Casinum, where an important pass was to be secured; but Hannibal's Carthaginian accent, not well-suited to Latin names, led the guide to mishear Casilinum instead of Casinum. The mistake was not discovered until the army had nearly reached the wrong location.

To be ignorant of any one of the following four or five principles is unworthy of a warlike leader.

When a prince who is ready for war attacks a strong nation, his skill as a leader comes from stopping the enemy from gathering their forces. He intimidates his opponents, and their allies are scared off from uniting against him.

[Mei Tao-ch'en offers one of the logical chains of thought that the Chinese are fond of: "When attacking a strong state, if you can separate its forces, you gain the advantage in strength; if you have the advantage in strength, you can intimidate the enemy; if you intimidate the enemy, neighboring states will become fearful; and if neighboring states are fearful, the enemy's allies will be stopped from joining her." The following interpretation gives an even stronger meaning: "If the powerful state is defeated before they can call on their allies, then the smaller states will hesitate and avoid bringing their forces together." Ch'en Hao and Chang Yu understand this in a very different way. Ch'en Hao says: "Even though a prince may be strong, if he attacks a large state, he won't have enough troops and will have to rely on outside help. If he ignores this and, with too much confidence in his own strength, tries to scare the enemy, he will certainly lose." Chang Yu explains it this way: "If we recklessly attack a large state, our own people will be unhappy and hesitant. And if our military power is clearly weaker than the enemy's, other leaders will be too scared to join us."]

So, he does not try to form alliances with everyone, nor does he help other states become stronger. He carries out his secret plans, keeping his enemies in fear.

[Li Ch'uan explains the thinking like this: Confident that his enemies won't join forces, "he can afford to turn down risky alliances and just focus on his own secret plans, with his reputation allowing him to do without external friendships."]

In this way, he can capture their cities and bring down their kingdoms.

[Even though this paragraph was written long before the state of Ch'in became a serious threat, it sums up well the strategy that the Six Chancellors used to pave the way for Ch'in's final victory under Shih Huang Ti. Chang Yu, expanding on his earlier note, thinks that Sun Tzŭ is criticizing this cold, selfish, and isolated approach.]

Bestow rewards without regard to rules,

[Wu Tzŭ, less wisely, says: "Let advancement be richly rewarded and retreat be heavily punished."]

Issue orders

[Literally, "hang" or post them up.] without regard to previous arrangements;["In order to prevent treachery," says Wang Hsi. The general meaning is made clear by Ts'ao Kung's quotation from the Ssu-ma Fa: "Give instructions only upon sighting the enemy; give rewards when you see worthy deeds." Ts'ao Kung paraphrases: "The final instructions you give to your army should not match those that were previously posted." Chang Yu simplifies this to "your plans should not be revealed in advance." And Chia Lin adds: "There should be no fixed rules in your arrangements." Not only is there risk in letting your plans be known, but war often requires reversing them at the last moment.] and you will be able to manage a whole army as though you were dealing with just one man. [Cf. supra, § 34.]

Confront your soldiers with the action itself; never let them know your plan.

[Literally, "do not tell them words," meaning do not give reasons for any order. Lord Mansfield once told a junior colleague to "give no reasons" for his decisions, and this rule applies even more to a general than to a judge.]

When the situation looks promising, show it to them; but when the outlook is bleak, tell them nothing.

Place your army in deadly peril, and it will survive; throw it into desperate situations, and it will come out safely.

[These words of Sun Tzŭ were once quoted by Han Hsin to explain the tactics he used in one of his most brilliant battles, mentioned earlier. In 204 B.C., Han Hsin was sent against the army of Chao, halting ten miles from the Ching-hsing pass, where the enemy had gathered in full strength. At midnight, he sent out 2000 light cavalry, each equipped with a red flag. Their orders were to pass through narrow defiles and secretly observe the enemy. "When the men of Chao see me retreating in full flight," Han Hsin said, "they will abandon their defenses and chase us. This will be your signal to rush in, pull down the Chao banners, and raise the red flags of Han instead." He then told his other officers: "The enemy holds a strong position and won't attack us until they see the standard and drums of the commander-in-chief, fearing I might retreat through the mountains." With this, he sent out a division of 10,000 men, ordering them to form a line of battle with their backs to the River Ti. Upon seeing this maneuver, the entire Chao army burst into laughter. By morning, Han Hsin raised his general's flag and marched out of the pass with drums beating, quickly engaging the enemy. A fierce battle followed, lasting for some time, until Han Hsin and his colleague,

Chang Ni, left the drums and flag on the battlefield and fled to the division by the river, where another intense fight was underway. The enemy rushed after them to claim the trophies, leaving their defenses exposed, but the two generals managed to join their army, which was fighting desperately. Now it was time for the 2000 horsemen to act. When they saw the men of Chao pursuing the fleeing forces, they galloped behind the abandoned fortifications, tore down the enemy's flags, and replaced them with the banners of Han. When the Chao army looked back during the chase and saw the red flags, they were struck with terror. Convinced that the Hans had overpowered their king, they panicked and scattered, despite their leader's attempts to stop them. Then the Han forces attacked from both sides, completely routing the Chao army, killing many and capturing the rest, including King Ya himself. After the battle, some of Han Hsin's officers approached him and said: "In the Art of War, we are taught to position troops with a hill or mound on the right rear and a river or marsh on the left front. Yet you ordered us to draw up with the river at our backs. How did you manage to win under such conditions?" The general replied: "I'm afraid you haven't studied the Art of War carefully enough. Does it not say, 'Plunge your army into desperate straits, and it will come off in safety; place it in deadly peril, and it will survive'? Had I followed the usual methods, I wouldn't have been able to bring my colleague around. As the Military Classic says, 'Swoop down on the marketplace and drive the men off to fight.' If I hadn't placed my troops where they had no choice but to fight for their lives, and instead allowed them to act freely, they would have scattered, and we couldn't have accomplished anything." The officers acknowledged the wisdom of his argument and said: "These are tactics beyond our own abilities."]

For it is precisely when a force finds itself in danger that it becomes capable of striking a blow for victory.

[Danger has a motivating effect.]

Success in warfare is achieved by carefully adapting to the enemy's intentions.

[Ts'ao Kung says: "Feign ignorance" by appearing to comply with the enemy's wishes. Chang Yu explains: "If the enemy shows a desire to advance, encourage him to do so; if he wishes to retreat, delay deliberately to allow him to carry out his plan." The goal is to make him overconfident and careless before launching our attack.]

By constantly keeping pressure on the enemy's flank,

[I understand this to mean "moving alongside the enemy in the same direction." Ts'ao Kung says: "Unite the troops and advance towards the enemy." But such a rearrangement of words is not defensible.] we will eventually succeed, [Literally, "after a thousand li."] in killing the enemy's commander. [This was always a significant aim in Chinese warfare.]

This is what it means to achieve something through sheer strategy.

On the day you take command, block the frontier passes, destroy the official tallies,

[These were tablets of bamboo or wood, half of which was used as a permit by an official. When returned within a set period, the gate could be opened for the traveler.] and stop all communication, [Whether to or from the enemy's territory.]

Be firm in the council-chamber,

[Show no weakness, and ensure your plans are approved by the ruler.] so that you can maintain control over the situation. [Mei Yao-ch'en interprets this to mean: Take the strictest measures to maintain secrecy in your discussions.]

If the enemy leaves an opening, you must charge through it.

Outsmart your opponent by seizing what he values most,

[See earlier, § 18.] and subtly manipulate the timing of his arrival at the battlefield. [Ch'en Hao explains: "If I seize a favorable position but the enemy doesn't show up, the advantage gained is meaningless. To control an important position, you must create a kind of 'appointment' with the enemy, tricking him into arriving there as well." Mei Yao-ch'en says this "appointment" can be made by using the enemy's own spies, who will bring back only the information we want them to have. Once we've cunningly revealed our plans, we can make sure, by starting after the enemy, that we arrive before him (VII. § 4). Starting later forces him to move there; arriving first allows us to capture the position without resistance. This supports Mei Yao-ch'en's reading of § 47.]

Walk the path guided by strategy,

[Chia Lin says: "Victory is all that matters, and this cannot be won by strictly following conventional rules." Unfortunately, this interpretation relies on weak authority, though it makes much more sense. As we know, Napoleon, according to the veterans of the old school whom he defeated, won his battles by breaking all the traditional rules of warfare.] and adapt to the enemy until the moment comes for a decisive battle. [Tu Mu says: "Follow the enemy's tactics until a favorable moment arises; then engage in a battle that will be conclusive."]

At first, show the reserve of a shy maiden until the enemy gives you an opening; then strike with the speed of a running hare, and it will be too late for the enemy to resist you.

[Though the hare is known for its timidity, Sun Tzŭ was clearly referring to its speed. The words have sometimes been interpreted to mean fleeing from the enemy as fast as a hare, but Tu Mu rightly rejects this idea.]

Chapter 12 - The Attack by Fire

Sun Tzŭ said: There are five ways to attack using fire. The first is to set fire to soldiers in their camp.

[Tu Mu agrees. Li Ch'uan adds: "Set the camp on fire, and kill the soldiers as they try to escape from the flames." Pan Ch'ao, on a diplomatic mission to the King of Shan-shan, found himself in great danger when an envoy from the Hsiung-nu, China's mortal enemies, unexpectedly arrived. During a meeting with his officers, he declared: "Nothing ventured, nothing gained! Our only option now is to attack the barbarians with fire under the cover of night, when they won't be able to see how many we are. Taking advantage of their panic, we can wipe them out, discourage the King, and achieve glory, ensuring the success of our mission." The officers suggested discussing the plan with the Intendant first, but Pan Ch'ao was outraged: "Today is the day our fate will be decided! The Intendant is a mere civilian and will be too scared when he hears our plan, leading to its exposure. Dying ingloriously is not the fate for brave warriors." The officers then agreed to follow his lead. That night, Pan Ch'ao and his small group approached the barbarian camp. A strong wind was blowing. Pan Ch'ao ordered ten men to hide behind the enemy barracks with drums, ready to make a loud noise when they saw the fire. The rest of his men, armed with bows and crossbows, were placed in ambush at the camp's gate. Pan Ch'ao set the camp on fire from the windward side, and immediately, the drums began to beat, and shouts filled the air. The Hsiung-nu ran out in panic. Pan Ch'ao personally killed three of them, while his men beheaded the envoy and thirty others. More than a hundred of the enemy perished in the flames. The next day, Pan Ch'ao, aware of the Intendant's concerns, assured him, "Although you didn't join us last night, I won't take sole credit for the success." This satisfied Kuo Hsun, and Pan Ch'ao presented the head of the barbarian envoy to the King of Shan-shan, causing fear throughout the kingdom. Pan Ch'ao calmed the situation by issuing a public proclamation, took the king's sons as hostages, and then reported his success to Tou Ku." *Hou Han Shu,* ch. 47, ff. 1, 2.]

The second is to burn stores.

[Tu Mu says: "Food, fuel, and fodder." During the Sui dynasty, to subdue the rebellious population of Kiangnan, Kao Keng advised Emperor Wen Ti to make periodic raids and burn their grain stores, a strategy that ultimately succeeded.]

The third is to burn baggage trains.

[An example is Ts'ao Ts'ao's destruction of Yuan Shao's wagons and supplies in 200 A.D.]

The fourth is to burn arsenals and magazines.

[Tu Mu explains that arsenals and magazines contain the same items, listing weapons, bullion, and clothing. See VII. § 11 for comparison.]

The fifth is to hurl fire into the enemy's camp.

[Tu Yu mentions in the *T'ung Tien*: "To drop fire into the enemy camp, dip arrowheads into a brazier to set them alight and then shoot them from powerful crossbows into the enemy's lines."]

In order to carry out an attack, we must have the necessary means available.

[T'sao Kung believes this refers to "traitors in the enemy's camp." However, Ch'en Hao more likely means: "We must have favorable circumstances in general, not just rely on traitors." Chia Lin adds: "We should take advantage of wind and dry weather."]

The material for raising fire should always be kept ready.

[Tu Mu suggests materials for starting a fire like "dry vegetation, reeds, brushwood, straw, grease, oil, etc." This is the material cause. Chang Yu adds: "Containers for hoarding fire and things for lighting fires."]

There is a proper season for making attacks with fire and specific days for starting a blaze.

The proper season is during very dry weather, and the specific days are when the moon is in the constellations of the Sieve, the Wall, the Wing, or the Crossbar;

[These correspond roughly to the 7th, 14th, 27th, and 28th of the Twenty-eight Stellar Mansions, which are Sagittarius, Pegasus, Crater, and Corvus.] because these four are all days when the wind rises. When attacking with fire, you must be prepared for five possible outcomes:

(1) When fire breaks out inside the enemy's camp, immediately launch an attack from outside.

(2) If a fire starts but the enemy's soldiers remain calm, wait and do not attack.

[The main goal of attacking with fire is to create confusion among the enemy. If that doesn't happen, it means the enemy is prepared for you. Therefore, caution is necessary.]

(3) When the flames reach their peak, follow up with an attack if possible; if not, stay where you are.

[Ts'ao Kung advises: "If you see an opportunity, advance; but if the difficulties seem too great, retreat."]

If it is possible to make an assault with fire from the outside, do not wait for it to break out within, but launch your attack at a favorable moment.

[Tu Mu explains that the previous sections referred to fire breaking out inside the enemy's camp, either by accident or through arson. He adds: "But if the enemy is camped in a waste area filled with grass, or if he has set up camp in a location that can easily be burned, we should attack with fire at any good opportunity instead of waiting for a fire to start within. Otherwise, the enemy might burn the surrounding vegetation themselves, rendering our efforts useless." The famous Li Ling once outsmarted a leader of the Hsiung-nu this way. The latter, taking advantage of a favorable wind, attempted to set fire to the Chinese general's camp, but found that all combustible vegetation had already been burned down. On the other hand, Po-ts'ai, a general of the Yellow Turban rebels, was badly defeated in 184 A.D. for neglecting this basic precaution. While leading a large army, he was besieging Ch'ang-she, which was defended by Huang-fu Sung. Although the garrison was small and nervous, Huang-fu Sung called his officers together and said: "In war, there are various indirect ways to attack, and numbers are not everything." [Here the commentator quotes Sun Tzŭ, V. §§ 5, 6, and 10.] "The rebels have set up camp in thick grass that will easily catch fire when the wind blows. If we set fire to it at night, they will panic, and we can attack from all sides, just like T'ien Tan did." [See page 90.] That night, a strong breeze arose, so Huang-fu Sung ordered his soldiers to bind reeds into torches and guard the city walls. Then, he sent out a group of brave men who sneaked through the enemy lines and started the fire with loud shouts and yells. At the same time, a bright light flared up from the city walls, and Huang-fu Sung, sounding the drums, led a swift charge, throwing the rebels into confusion and sending them fleeing." *Hou Han Shu,* ch. 71.]

When you start a fire, make sure you are upwind from it. Do not attack from the downwind side.

[Chang Yu, following Tu Yu, explains: "When you start a fire, the enemy will retreat away from it; if you block their retreat and attack, they will fight desperately, which will not lead to your success." Tu Mu offers a simpler explanation: "If the wind is blowing from the east, begin burning to the east of the enemy and follow up your attack from that direction. If you start the fire on the east side and attack from the west, both you and the enemy will suffer."]

A wind that rises during the day lasts long, but a night breeze dies down quickly.

[Lao Tzŭ says: "A violent wind does not last the space of a morning." (Tao Te Ching, chap. 23.) Mei Yao-ch'en and Wang Hsi explain: "A daytime breeze fades at nightfall, and a night breeze ends at daybreak.

This is usually the case." While this observation may be accurate, how this applies in the context is not immediately clear.]

In every army, the five developments related to fire must be understood, the movements of the stars calculated, and attention paid to the proper days.

[Tu Mu says: "We must calculate the paths of the stars and watch for the days when wind will rise before launching a fire attack." Chang Yu seems to interpret the text differently, suggesting: "We must not only know how to attack our opponents with fire but also guard against similar attacks from them."]

Those who use fire as a tool for attacking show intelligence, while those who use water as a tool for attacking gain additional strength.

By means of water, an enemy may be intercepted, but not stripped of all his possessions.

[Ts'ao Kung comments: "We can only obstruct the enemy's path or divide his forces, but we cannot wipe out all his stores." Water can be helpful, but it lacks the overwhelming destructive power of fire. This, Chang Yu concludes, is why water is dismissed in just a few lines, while fire attacks are discussed in detail. Wu Tzŭ (ch. 4) remarks: "If an army is camped on low-lying marshy ground, where water can't drain away, and where rainfall is heavy, it may be flooded. If an army is camped in wild marshlands overgrown with weeds and brambles, and frequently visited by gales, it may be wiped out by fire."]

Unhappy is the fate of one who tries to win his battles and succeed in his attacks without fostering a spirit of initiative; for the result is wasted time and general stagnation.

[This is one of the most puzzling passages in Sun Tzŭ. Ts'ao Kung says: "Rewards for good service should not be delayed even for a single day." Tu Mu adds: "If you don't seize the opportunity to advance and reward those who deserve it, your subordinates will not follow your orders, and disaster will follow." However, I prefer the interpretation suggested by Mei Yao-ch'en, whose words I will quote: "Those who want to ensure success in their battles and attacks must seize favorable opportunities when they arise and not shy away from bold measures. That means they must use such means of attack as fire, water, and the like. What they must avoid, which will lead to failure, is sitting still and merely holding on to the advantages they have already gained."]

Hence the saying: The enlightened ruler plans well in advance; the capable general builds up his resources.

[Tu Mu quotes from the *San Lueh,* ch. 2: "The warlike prince controls his soldiers through his authority, unites them through trust, and makes them serve through rewards. If trust fades, there will be disorder; if rewards are insufficient, orders will not be obeyed."]

Move not unless you see an advantage; use not your troops unless there is something to be gained; fight not unless the position is critical.

[Sun Tzŭ may seem overly cautious at times, but he never goes as far as the passage in the *Tao Te Ching,* ch. 69: "I dare not take the initiative but prefer to act defensively; I dare not advance an inch but prefer to retreat a foot."]

No ruler should send troops into the field merely to satisfy personal anger; no general should fight a battle out of resentment.

If it benefits you, make a forward move; if not, stay where you are.

[This repeats from XI. § 17. It feels like an interpolation here because § 20 clearly follows from § 18.]

Anger may eventually turn into gladness; frustration may be replaced by contentment.

But a kingdom once destroyed can never be restored;

[The Wu State serves as a sad example of this saying.] nor can the dead ever be brought back to life. Therefore, the enlightened ruler is cautious, and the wise general is full of care. This is the way to keep a country at peace and an army intact.

["Unless you enter the tiger's lair, you cannot catch its cubs."]

Chapter 13 - The Use of Spies

Sun Tzŭ said: Raising an army of a hundred thousand men and marching them over long distances causes heavy losses to the people and drains the State's resources. The daily cost will amount to a thousand ounces of silver.

[Cf. II. §§ 1, 13, 14.]

There will be unrest both at home and abroad, and men will collapse from exhaustion along the highways.

[Cf. *Tao Te Ching,* ch. 30: "Where troops have been stationed, thorns and brambles spring up." Chang Yu notes: "We are reminded of the saying: 'On serious ground, gather in plunder.' So why does transport cause such exhaustion on the highways?—The answer lies in the fact that it is not just food but all sorts of munitions that must be transported to the army. Additionally, the command to 'forage on the enemy' means that, when deeply engaged in enemy territory, food shortages must be anticipated. Therefore, while not entirely dependent on the enemy for supplies, we must forage to ensure a continuous flow. Moreover, in places like salt deserts, where provisions are unavailable, supplies from home become indispensable."]

As many as seven hundred thousand families will be hindered in their work.

[Mei Yao-ch'en comments: "There will be a shortage of men to work the fields." The reference is to the system of dividing land into nine parts, with the central plot farmed for the State by the tenants of the other eight plots. It was here, as Tu Mu notes, that the families built their cottages and shared a common well. [See II. § 12, note.] During wartime, one family had to serve in the army, while the other seven provided support. Therefore, when 100,000 men were conscripted (with one able-bodied soldier per family), the agricultural work of 700,000 families would be affected.]

Hostile armies may face each other for years, striving for a victory that is decided in a single day. Given this, to remain ignorant of the enemy's condition simply because one begrudges the cost of a hundred ounces of silver for rewards and payments

["For spies" is implied here, though it is not explicitly mentioned to maintain the effect of this elaborate introduction.] is the height of inhumanity.

[Sun Tzŭ's argument is quite clever. He starts by acknowledging the immense misery and staggering cost in lives and resources that war brings. If you remain uninformed about the enemy's situation and fail to strike at the right moment, a war can drag on for years. The only way to get this information is by employing spies, and reliable spies cannot be found unless they are well paid. It is false economy to begrudge such a small amount when each additional day of war costs vastly more. This burden falls hardest on the poor, so neglecting the use of spies is, in Sun Tzŭ's view, nothing less than a crime against humanity.]

One who acts in this way is no leader of men, no true support to his sovereign, and no master of victory.

[This notion, that the ultimate goal of war is peace, has deep roots in the Chinese national temperament. Even as far back as 597 B.C., Prince Chuang of the Ch'u State said: "The [Chinese] character for 'prowess' is formed by the characters for 'to stay' and 'a spear' (the cessation of hostilities). Military prowess is seen in the suppression of cruelty, the laying down of weapons, upholding the mandate of Heaven, establishing merit, bringing happiness to the people, promoting harmony among the princes, and spreading wealth."]

Thus, what enables the wise sovereign and the good general to strike and conquer, achieving things beyond the reach of ordinary men, is foreknowledge.

[That is, understanding the enemy's plans and intentions.]

Now, this foreknowledge cannot be gained from spirits; it cannot be derived from experience,

[Tu Mu explains: "[Knowledge of the enemy] cannot be obtained by reasoning from similar cases."] nor can it be deduced through calculation. [Li Ch'uan notes: "Quantities like length, breadth, distance, and magnitude can be determined mathematically, but human actions cannot be calculated in the same way."]

Knowledge of the enemy's plans can only be obtained from other men.

[Mei Yao-ch'en adds an interesting point: "Divination can provide knowledge of the spirit-world; inductive reasoning can reveal truths in natural science; and mathematical calculation can verify the laws of the universe. But the enemy's plans can only be learned through spies, and spies alone."]

Hence the use of spies, of whom there are five types: (1) Local spies; (2) inward spies; (3) converted spies; (4) doomed spies; (5) surviving spies.

When all five types of spies are working together, no one can unravel the secret system. This is called "divine manipulation of the threads." It is the sovereign's most valuable skill.

[Cromwell, one of the greatest and most practical cavalry leaders, had officers called 'scout masters,' whose task was to gather all possible intelligence regarding the enemy through scouts and spies. Much of his success in warfare was due to the prior knowledge of the enemy's movements gained in this way.]

Having local spies means using the inhabitants of a region.

[Tu Mu advises: "In the enemy's country, win people over through kind treatment and use them as spies."]

Having inward spies means using officials of the enemy.

[Tu Mu lists several groups likely to be useful in this regard: "Worthy men who have been disgraced, criminals who have been punished, favorite concubines greedy for gold, men frustrated with being in subordinate positions or passed over for promotions, others hoping for their side's defeat so they can showcase their talents, and turncoats who always try to keep a foot in both camps. Officials of these types should be secretly approached and won over with rich gifts. In this way, you can discover the state of affairs in the enemy's country, learn their plans, and also cause discord between the ruler and his ministers." However, dealing with inward spies requires extreme caution, as illustrated by an incident related by Ho Shih: "Lo Shang, Governor of I-Chou, sent his general Wei Po to attack the rebel Li Hsiung of Shu in his stronghold at P'i. After several victories and defeats on both sides, Li Hsiung employed the services of a certain P'o-t'ai, a native of Wu-tu. He had P'o-t'ai whipped until blood flowed, then sent him to deceive Lo Shang by pretending to cooperate from inside the city and promising to light a fire signal for a coordinated assault. Lo Shang trusted these promises, sent out his best troops, and ordered Wei Po and others to attack when P'o-t'ai signaled. Meanwhile, Li Hsiung's general, Li Hsiang, prepared an ambush along their path. P'o-t'ai then raised long scaling ladders against the city walls and lit the signal fire. Wei Po's men rushed in upon seeing the signal, climbed the ladders, and were pulled up by ropes. More than a hundred of Lo Shang's soldiers entered the city, where they were immediately beheaded. Li Hsiung then charged with his full forces, both inside and outside the city, and completely routed the enemy." This occurred in 303 A.D. Though Ho Shih does not provide his source, it is not mentioned in the biographies of Li Hsiung or his father, Li T'e, in *Chin Shu,* ch. 120, 121.]

Having converted spies means capturing the enemy's spies and using them for our own purposes.

[This involves offering them large bribes and making generous promises to turn them against their original side, so they will send false information back to the enemy and spy on their own people. Another approach, mentioned by Hsiao Shih-hsien, is to pretend that we haven't caught on to the spy, allowing him to leave with a false understanding of what is happening. Some commentators accept this as an alternative interpretation, but it's not what Sun Tzŭ intended, as shown by his later comments on treating the converted spy well. Ho Shih gives three examples of successful use of converted spies: (1) T'ien Tan in his defense of Chi-mo, (2) Chao She on his march to O-yu, and (3) Fan Chu in 260 B.C., when Lien P'o was conducting a defensive campaign against Ch'in. The King of Chao, unhappy with Lien P'o's slow and cautious methods, listened to reports from spies who had secretly switched sides and were already being paid by Fan Chu. The spies said, "The only concern Ch'in has is if Chao Kua becomes general. They see Lien P'o as an easy target who will be defeated eventually." Chao Kua, the son of the famous general Chao She, had been obsessed with war and strategy since childhood, believing no one could defeat him. His father, worried about his arrogance, warned that if Kua ever became a general, he would ruin the army of Chao. Despite warnings from his mother and the statesman Lin Hsiang-ju, Chao Kua was appointed to replace Lien P'o. He proved no match for the skilled general Po Ch'i and the mighty Ch'in army. His army was split, his supply lines were cut, and after a 46-day resistance, during which his starving soldiers resorted to cannibalism, he was killed by an arrow, and his entire force, reportedly 400,000 men, was slaughtered.]

Having doomed spies means openly doing certain things to deceive the enemy and letting our own spies know about it so they can report back.

[Tu Yu explains it best: "We deliberately do things to fool our own spies into thinking they've uncovered real secrets. When they are caught by the enemy, they will give false reports, causing the enemy to prepare for something that won't happen." Once the enemy realizes the deception, the spies will be executed. Ho Shih gives the example of prisoners released by Pan Ch'ao during his campaign against Yarkand. He also mentions T'ang Chien, who was sent by T'ai Tsung in 630 A.D. to lull the Turkish Kahn Chieh-li into a false sense of security until Li Ching could launch a surprise attack. Some say the Turks killed T'ang Chien in revenge, but both the old and new T'ang histories record that he escaped and lived until 656. Li I-chi played a similar role in 203 B.C., when sent by the King of Han to negotiate with Ch'i. Li I-chi may be a more fitting example of a doomed spy, as the King of Ch'i, feeling betrayed after an unexpected attack by Han Hsin, had Li I-chi boiled alive.]

Surviving spies are those who return with information from the enemy's camp.

[These are the typical spies, forming a regular part of the army. Tu Mu says: "A surviving spy must be intelligent but appear foolish; he should look shabby on the outside but possess a strong will. He must be active, tough, physically strong, and brave; accustomed to doing dirty work, able to endure hunger and cold, and capable of handling shame and humiliation." Ho Shih tells a story about Ta'hsi Wu of the Sui dynasty: "When he was governor of Eastern Ch'in, Shen-wu of Ch'i launched an attack on Sha-yuan. Emperor T'ai Tsu sent Ta'hsi Wu to spy on the enemy, accompanied by two others. They rode on horseback, wearing the enemy's uniform. After nightfall, they dismounted a few hundred feet from the enemy's camp and sneaked closer to listen. They managed to overhear the army's passwords. Then they got back on their horses and, pretending to be night watchmen, boldly rode through the camp. Several times, they even punished soldiers who were breaking the rules, beating them as if they were enforcing discipline! This way, they gathered detailed information about the enemy's position and returned to report. The Emperor was so impressed by their intelligence that he used it to achieve a major victory over the enemy."]

Hence, none in the entire army should be more closely connected with than spies.

[Tu Mu and Mei Yao-ch'en note that spies have the privilege of entering even the general's private tent.]

No one should be rewarded more generously, and no other work should be kept more secret.

[Tu Mu adds that all communication with spies should be done "mouth-to-ear," in utmost secrecy.

The following advice on spies can be quoted from Turenne, who used them more than any previous commander: “Spies work for those who pay them the most. A commander who pays poorly will never be well-served. They should remain unknown to others, and they should not know one another. When they propose something important, secure their loyalty by holding them or their families as hostages for their faithfulness. Only share with them what is absolutely necessary for them to know.”]

Spies cannot be effectively used without a certain intuitive sagacity.

[Mei Yao-ch’en says: “To use them well, you must be able to distinguish truth from lies and recognize honesty from deceit.” Wang Hsi interprets this more as “intuitive perception” and “practical intelligence.” Tu Mu, however, strangely attributes these qualities to the spies themselves: “Before employing spies, we must confirm their integrity and assess their experience and skills.” But he adds: “A bold face and a cunning mind are more dangerous than mountains or rivers; it takes a genius to see through them.” This leaves some uncertainty as to his true view of the passage.]

They cannot be properly managed without benevolence and straightforwardness.

[Chang Yu says: “After attracting spies with good offers, you must treat them with complete sincerity, so they will serve you with full dedication."]

Without subtle ingenuity, one cannot be sure of the accuracy of their reports.

[Mei Yao-ch'en warns: "Beware of the possibility that spies might defect to the enemy."]

Be subtle! Be subtle! And use your spies for all kinds of tasks.

If a spy leaks a secret before the time is right, he must be executed along with the person who received the information.

[The literal translation is: "If spy matters are heard before [our plans] are carried out," etc. Sun Tzŭ's point is that the spy is executed as punishment for revealing the secret, while the other person is killed, as Ch'en Hao explains, "to keep his mouth shut" and prevent further leaks. If the information has already been shared with others, this would be ineffective. Sun Tzŭ's advice may seem harsh, though Tu Mu defends it, saying the recipient deserves punishment because he must have pressured the spy into revealing the secret.]

Whether the goal is to defeat an army, storm a city, or assassinate a leader, it is crucial to start by learning the names of the attendants, aides-de-camp,

[Literally "visitors," referring to those who supply the general with information, requiring regular meetings with him.] the doorkeepers, and sentries of the general in command. Our spies must be assigned to find out these details. [This would be the first step toward determining whether any of these key figures can be bribed.]

The enemy's spies who come to spy on us must be identified, tempted with bribes, and then won over and treated well. This way, they become converted spies and can work for us.

It is through the information provided by the converted spy that we can recruit and use local and inward spies.

[Tu Yu explains: "By converting the enemy's spies, we learn the true state of the enemy." Chang Yu adds: "We must entice the converted spy into our service because he knows which local inhabitants are greedy for profit and which officials are open to corruption."]

It is also through the converted spy's information that we can use doomed spies to send false reports to the enemy.

[Chang Yu says, "The converted spy knows the best ways to deceive the enemy."]

Finally, the converted spy's information allows us to use the surviving spy on special occasions.

The ultimate purpose of all five types of spies is to gain knowledge of the enemy; and this knowledge primarily comes from the converted spy.

[As outlined in §§ 22-24. The converted spy not only provides direct information but also makes it possible to effectively employ the other types of spies.]

Therefore, it is crucial to treat the converted spy with the greatest generosity.

Of old, the rise of the Yin dynasty

[Sun Tzŭ is referring to the Shang dynasty, founded in 1766 B.C., which was later renamed Yin by P'an Keng in 1401.] was due to I Chih [Also known as I Yin, the famous general and statesman who played a key role in Ch'eng T'ang's campaign against Chieh Kuei.] who had served under the Hsia. Likewise, the rise of the Chou dynasty was due to Lü Ya [Lü Shang, who rose to prominence under the tyrant Chou Hsin, later helped to overthrow him. He is widely known as T'ai Kung, a title given to him by Wen Wang, and is said to have authored a treatise on war, though it has been wrongly identified with the *Liu T'ao.*] who had served under the Yin. [The Chinese wording here is less precise than this translation, and the commentaries are not clear. However, in the context, it seems likely that Sun Tzŭ is presenting I Chih and Lü Ya as examples of converted spies or something similar. His point is that the Hsia and Yin dynasties fell because these former ministers had intimate knowledge of their weaknesses, which they shared with the opposing side. Mei Yao-ch'en objects to this interpretation, saying: "I Yin and Lü Ya were not traitors. The Hsia dynasty failed to employ I Yin, so the Yin did. The Yin dynasty failed to employ Lü Ya, so the Chou did. Their great deeds were for the benefit of the people." Ho Shih is also offended: "How could divinely inspired men like I and Lü have been mere spies? Sun Tzŭ is not suggesting that they were spies, but rather that using spies requires the highest level of intelligence, which people like I and Lü possessed. That is why they are mentioned here." Ho Shih believes they are referenced for their wisdom in using spies, but this interpretation is weak.]

Hence, only the enlightened ruler and the wise general will use the highest intelligence in the army for spying, and by doing so, they achieve great results.

[Tu Mu concludes with a note of caution: "Just as water, which can carry a boat across a river, can also sink it, so relying on spies can bring great success but also lead to disaster."]

Spies are a crucial part of warfare because the movement of the army depends on them.

Thank You for Reading

You've Just Read a Piece of the Greatest Library Ever Rebuilt

Thank you for reading.

This book is one of thousands we're restoring, reimagining, and translating as part of the **Modern Library of Alexandria** — a global movement to preserve and share humanity's most important ideas.

What was once lost to fire and time is now rising again — not just as memory, but as living, breathing knowledge, freely accessible to all.

What You Can Do Next:

- **Keep Reading** - Explore more legendary works in print, audiobook, or digital at LibraryofAlexandria.com.
- **Build Your Own Library** - Every title is available at true printing cost — paperback, hardcover, or collector's boxset.
- **Spread the Light** - Share this book. Support the mission to translate every timeless work into every language.

By finishing this book, you've already taken part in something extraordinary.

Join us at LibraryofAlexandria.com

Together, we're rebuilding the greatest library the world has ever known.

With gratitude,

The Modern Library of Alexandria Team

Visit:

www.libraryofalexandria.com

Or scan the code below:

www.ingramcontent.com/pod-product-compliance
Lightning Source LLC
Chambersburg PA
CBHW010139030826
48979CB00023B/1046

* 9 7 8 1 8 0 6 9 8 9 7 8 2 *